# RUNNING
## WITH
# HOUSE
# MONEY

### How I Turned Credit into Cashflow, Real Estate, and Free Travel

## BY LEE A. PATTERSON

## DISCLAIMER

The advice contained in this material might not be suitable for everyone. The authors designed the information to present their opinion about the subject matter. The reader must carefully investigate all aspects of any business decision before committing to him or herself. The authors obtained the information contained herein from sources they believe to be reliable and from their own personal experiences, but they neither imply nor intend any guarantee of accuracy. The authors are not in the business of giving legal, accounting, or any other type of professional advice. Should the reader need such advice, he or she must seek services from a competent professional. The authors particularly disclaims any liability, loss, or risk taken by individuals who directly or indirectly act on the information contained herein. The authors believe the advice presented here is sound, but readers cannot hold them responsible for either the actions they take, or the risk taken by individuals who directly or indirectly act on the information contained herein.

Published by 1Brick Publishing
Printed in the United States
Copyright © 2025 by Lee A. Patterson
ISBN 979-8898560188

# DEDICATION

To the kid on the Greyhound bus with nothing but a box and a dream— this book is for you.

To my mother, who showed me how to make something out of nothing and never let struggle define us.

To my father, whose absence taught me how to stand on my own. And to every student, runner, hustler, or underdog who ever felt like they didn't have enough to start— you have everything you need inside of you.

To my teammate Mike who was my first mentor, my early morning running partners and student-athletes at Clarke Central High School who's taken this journey with me.

And to my first investor who believed in me, and every student I've taught the game of real estate and credit to.

This journey isn't about perfection. It's about persistence, systems, and faith. Thank you to everyone who believed in me before I believed in myself.

We don't just buy houses—we buy freedom.

# Dedication Request

Please share this book with anyone who's ever believed they were one decision, one strategy, or one system away from changing their life.

Share it with the dreamers, the doers, and especially the ones who've been counted out. Let this be the blueprint that turns credit into keys—and hustle into legacy.

# Table of Contents

# INTRODUCTION

# The Other Side of Risk

I'm sitting in my car in Athens, Georgia, looking across the street at a house I own. It's not much to look at—just a simple rental property in a college town. But what makes this moment surreal is that I'm parked here because I'm about to coach track practice at the local high school, mentoring kids who live in the same neighborhood where I now collect rent checks.

Twenty-eight years ago, I left Longview, Texas with everything I owned stuffed into a box about twice as wide as me. I was on a Greyhound bus, headed to a junior college in Garden City, Kansas—a place so remote you could drive to Colorado faster than you could get to the nearest big city. I had no credit, mediocre grades, and a track scholarship that was more hope than guarantee.

Today, I own multiple properties in Georgia, land back home in Texas, and a residence in Dubai. I've traveled to over 50 countries, many of them in first class, using points I earned from the same credit cards I used to buy those properties. And I did it all without using my own money.

This isn't a rags-to-riches fantasy. This is a blueprint.

See, somewhere along the way, we've been sold a lie about money. We've been told you need money to make money. That real estate is for people with trust funds and perfect credit scores. That you should be afraid of debt and hide from credit cards like they're financial kryptonite.

But here's what I learned running cross country in 99-degree Texas heat, grinding through two years at a JUCO in the middle of nowhere, and eventually finding my way to the University of Georgia: **the biggest risk in life is not taking one.**

I tell people all the time—I took that risk, and this is what the other side of risk looks like. Sitting here, talking to you through these pages, teaching others how to run their own race from credit to keys, from funding to freedom.

**You Don't Need Perfect to Start**

Let me be clear about something right up front: I wasn't the smartest kid in any room. I got my college degree just trying to stay eligible to run track, and I promise you I've never used that degree a day in my life. My credit was trash. My bank account was emptier than a small-town movie theater on a Tuesday night.

But I had something more valuable than perfect circumstances—I had faith and I was too stubborn to quit.

I grew up broke, but I was never poor. There's a difference. Broke is your situation; poor is your mindset. My grandparents were entrepreneurs selling snow cones and candy. My family ran a soul food restaurant where we all worked our first jobs. We grew our own vegetables and went fishing for dinner, not for fun. But even when the lights got cut off and we had to light candles, I knew in my spirit that this was temporary.

The good book says if we can believe it, we can achieve it. And I chose to believe in something bigger than my current situation.

## The System They Don't Want You to Know

Here's what blew my mind when I started learning about real estate and business funding: the same banks that wouldn't give me a loan for a decent used car were ready to hand me six figures in credit once I understood how the game really worked.

Business credit isn't just about your score—it's about your entire profile. Personal credit can be rebuilt using five simple factors. And once you understand how to leverage other people's money (OPM), you never have to wait for your own money to catch up to your dreams.

I've literally used credit cards to purchase real estate in Dubai. I've earned enough travel points from my property purchases and renovations to fly first class around the world. I've automated my rental properties so thoroughly that I don't even go to closings anymore—everything gets wired directly to my account.

But this isn't about getting rich quick. This is about getting rich *right*.

## What This Book Will Do for You

*House Money* isn't just my story—it's your instruction manual. Over the next 13 chapters, I'm going to walk you through the exact system I used to go from that box on the Greyhound bus to owning property on three continents.

You'll learn:

- How to rebuild and leverage your credit, even if it's currently terrible
- The science of getting funded without tax returns, bank statements, or traditional documentation
- How to find, analyze, and purchase income-producing real estate using other people's money
- The automation systems that gave me time freedom to coach, create content, and travel the world
- Travel hacking strategies that turn your business expenses into first-class flights and five-star hotels
- How to scale from your first property to an international portfolio

But more than the tactics, you'll discover the mindset shift that changes everything: **wealth starts in your mind first, not in your pocket.**

### Your Race Starts Now

I want you to understand something: I'm not special. I'm not a genius. I didn't inherit money or connections or some secret knowledge passed down through generations of wealth.

What I did have was a mentor who told me something that changed my life: "If you don't learn how to leverage money, you will work for somebody who will."

That stuck with me. And now I'm passing it on to you.

Every day I see people my age or younger driving to jobs they hate, working for bosses who don't appreciate them, living paycheck to paycheck even though they make decent money. They're afraid to take risks because they think their current situation is safer than the unknown.

But here's the truth: your current situation is only safe if you're satisfied with it staying exactly the same forever.

## The Time is Now

If you're reading this, you're probably in one of three places:

1.  You're just starting out, maybe with bad credit and big dreams, wondering if real estate is even possible for someone like you.
2.  You're already making decent money but you're tired of trading time for dollars, and you want to build something that works even when you're not.
3.  You've got some real estate experience but you're stuck trying to scale because you keep running out of money for down payments.

Wherever you are, this book meets you there. Because the same principles that took me from a JUCO track athlete to a global real estate investor will work for anyone willing to learn the system and put in the work.

I like to say I'm a man of God, a man of faith, and a man of the people. But I'm also a man who believes that knowledge without action is just entertainment. So as we go through this journey together, I don't just want you to be inspired—I want you to be equipped.

Every chapter ends with "House Money Hacks"—specific, actionable steps you can take immediately. I'll share the exact credit cards I use, the funding sources I tap, the property management systems I've built, and the travel strategies that have taken me to over 50 countries.

But most importantly, I'll share the mindset that makes it all possible.

**Welcome to Your Financial Freedom**

See, the thing about running track is that it taught me something crucial: you're not racing against anybody else. You're racing against your own limitations, your own excuses, your own fears.

The person who wins is the person who decides to keep running when everyone else gets tired.

So welcome to *House Money*. Welcome to the other side of risk. Welcome to your race from credit to keys, from funding to freedom.

Let's get started.

*"I might have grew up broke, but I ain't never been poor, right? Because the good book says God owns it all. He got it all. And if we can believe it, we can achieve it."*

— Lee A. Patterson
Athens, Georgia

# Part I:
# The Foundation

# CHAPTER 1

## The Box and the Bus

The box was cardboard, brown, and beat up from being moved around too much. It was about twice as wide as me, which wasn't saying much since I was 5'10" and maybe 155 pounds soaking wet. But that box contained everything I owned in the world: two pair of pants, a couple of shorts, two pair of shoes—one I had on my feet—and a winter jacket that I prayed would be enough for wherever I was headed.

I was sitting on a Greyhound bus at 18 years old, leaving Longview, Texas, with no clear idea of what I was getting myself into. All I knew was that I had to get out.

Growing up in East Texas, you learn early that there's a difference between being broke and being poor. We were definitely broke—lights getting cut off, using candles for dinner, government assistance, growing our own vegetables in the backyard because grocery money was tight. But we were never poor in spirit.

My grandparents were entrepreneurs before I even knew what the word meant. They sold snow cones and candy to kids in the neighborhood. My family ran a restaurant where all of us got our first jobs. We learned early that if you wanted something, you had to work for it. If you wanted to eat, sometimes you had to catch it yourself—I'm talking about fishing for dinner, not for sport.

But the thing about growing up like that is it gives you hunger. Real hunger. Not just for food, but for something better.

## The Moment Everything Changed

I'll never forget the moment I knew I had to leave Texas. I was probably 16, hanging around my older brother's barbershop where he cut hair. All kinds of people came through there—folks from the neighborhood, guys who had graduated a few years ahead of me, players coming back from college.

That's when I saw them.

These dudes would roll up in fresh rides, wearing Nike gear that still had the tags on it, talking about their scholarships and their schools. They'd get their hair cut and tell stories about places I'd only seen on TV during March Madness. Schools with names like Georgia, California, Ohio State, Arkansas, Alabama—places that seemed like they were on a different planet from Longview.

I remember thinking, "Man, that's what I want. That's my way out."

The problem was, I was 5'10" trying to make it in basketball. Let me put this in perspective for you—in Texas high school basketball, being under 6 feet is like bringing a spoon to a gunfight. I had heart, I had hustle, but I didn't have height.

My track coach was honest with me, and I appreciate him for that now. He sat me down one day after practice and said, "Lee, I'll be straight with you, bro. You ain't going nowhere with basketball, being the size you are and with what you got. But they give scholarships for running."

Running? Man, I'm going to be honest with you—I thought he was crazy. You could tell a black person to run a mile or run four laps (one mile), and which one you think we're going to choose? We're going to choose the four laps every time. Anything with the word "mile" in it, was a no go.

My basketball coach had a guy come to our basketball practice who had graduated four years prior from my high school and had run cross country at the University of Arkansas. This dude came in talking about full scholarships, room and board, the whole nine.

## Sometimes Your Backup Plan Becomes Your Main Plan

I'll never forget that first day trying out for cross country. It was 99 degrees in Texas—the kind of heat that makes you question your life choices. Coach took me on a run, and I'm not going to lie, it wasn't easy. But it wasn't impossible either.

What I discovered about running was something that would change my entire approach to life: **it was all on me.**

In basketball, you need your teammates to pass you the ball. You need refs to make fair calls. You need coaches to put you in the right position. But running? Running was 100% in my control. It didn't matter what color I was, how tall I was, or how much money my family had. If I put in the work, I would get better.

I understood right away that this was something I had control over. And for a kid who had felt powerless in a lot of areas of his life, that control was everything.

Plus, I had heard about the 10,000-hour rule by then. The idea that if you work at something for 10,000 hours, you can master it. I figured if I could get good enough at running to earn a scholarship, I could get good enough at anything else I set my mind to.

## The Academic Reality Check

Here's the thing they don't tell you about getting a college scholarship when you're focusing all your energy on sports: you still need to qualify academically. And let me just say, school was never my strongest suit.

I was passing my classes, but just enough to graduate and stay eligible. To get into most universities, you need a certain ACT or SAT score. I took the ACT one last time when we drove down to Texas A&M. At that point, I would have gone anywhere to get out of Longview.

I needed a 21. I scored a 20.

One point. One. Point.

I remember sitting in that testing room thinking, "This is it. This is what's going to keep me in Longview forever." But my coach had a backup plan. He had already connected with a coach at a junior college in Garden City, Kansas.

"You can go there," he told me, "get your grades right, keep running, and transfer to a bigger school in two years."

The next day, I was on a Greyhound bus.

## Everything I Owned

Let me paint the picture for you. Garden City, Kansas is so far west, you can drive to Colorado in about an hour. It's in the middle of absolutely nowhere. I'm talking about a place where the biggest entertainment on the weekend is driving to the Walmart in the next town over.

I was on that bus for 15 hours, and somewhere along the way, I met three other guys who were all headed to the same place. All of us from Texas, all of us with the same dream of using junior college as a stepping stone to something bigger.

We're looking around at each other like, "Man, what have we done?"

But here's the thing—I was excited. I know that sounds crazy, sitting on a Greyhound bus with everything you own in a cardboard box, headed to the middle of nowhere Kansas. But for the first time in my life, I felt like I was in control of my own story.

See, up until that moment, everything had been happening *to* me. I was born into the family I was born into, in the town I was born into, with the circumstances I was born into. But climbing on that bus was the first choice I made that was completely about creating the life I wanted to live.

## The Courage to Be Uncomfortable

Garden City Junior College was culture shock in every possible way. It was cold—Texas cold and Kansas cold are two completely different animals. I experienced snow for the very first time. It was isolated—you couldn't even see another building from most places on campus. And the population was tiny compared to what I was used to.

But it was also opportunity.

I ran cross country in the fall and track in the spring, which kept me busy year-round. The athletics program was actually pretty solid—they had sent guys to SEC schools, Big 12 schools, places I had dreamed about watching on TV.

More importantly, I was learning discipline in a way I never had before. When you're running 6-8 miles a day in Kansas winter, you learn real quick that motivation is temporary but discipline is permanent. You learn that success isn't about feeling like doing something—it's about doing it whether you feel like it or not.

I was also learning about delayed gratification. Everything in junior college was about what came next. The grades you were earning, the times you were running, the relationships you were building—it was all preparation for the transfer.

And I was hungry. Not just physically (though the cafeteria food was questionable), but hungry for something more. Every day I was running, I was thinking about where I wanted to end up. Every night I was studying (more than I ever had in high school), I was thinking about the schools that might want me.

## The Two-Year Plan

I attacked junior college like I was training for the Olympics. I didn't even go to summer school—I was so focused that I calculated exactly how many credit hours I needed to graduate and divided them evenly between four semesters. I was getting out of there as fast as possible.

The running was going well. My times were dropping. My grades were improving. And coaches from four-year schools were starting to pay attention.

But the real education was happening outside the classroom and off the track. I was learning how to be independent. How to manage my time. How to make decisions without my family there to guide me. How to be comfortable being uncomfortable.

Most importantly, I was learning that I could bet on myself and win.

## The Phone Call That Changed Everything

Halfway through my first year, my roommate got a call from a coach at the University of Georgia. He was from a town right next to Longview, so we had connected over being homesick Texans stuck in Kansas.

After he hung up, he looked at me and said, "Man, I'm going to Georgia. You should come too."

Georgia? I'm not going to lie—I thought the University of Georgia was in Atlanta. I thought I'd be in the big city, experiencing culture and night-life and all the things you see in movies about college.

But the opportunity was real. The coach was interested. My times qualified. My grades were finally good enough.

So I filled out the application, sent my transcripts, and waited.

## The Lesson in the Box

Looking back now, sitting here in Athens, Georgia, owning property in the same town where I came to college, I realize that box taught me something crucial about building wealth: **you don't need much to start, but you need to start.**

That box represented everything I thought I needed to succeed. But the real assets I was carrying weren't in the box—they were in my head and my heart. The willingness to be uncomfortable. The discipline to keep running when it hurt. The faith that something better was waiting if I was willing to work for it.

These are the same qualities I use today in real estate. The same mindset that got me on that Greyhound bus is the same mindset that helps me pull the trigger on property deals, apply for business credit, and take calculated risks that most people are afraid to take.

See, wealth building isn't really about having money to start. It's about having the courage to start with whatever you have and the discipline to keep going until you have what you want.

That box taught me that possessions don't make you wealthy—possibilities do.

## House Money Hack: Start With What You Have

Here's what I want you to understand: you don't need perfect circumstances to begin building wealth. You don't need a trust fund, perfect credit, or a detailed five-year plan.

You need three things:

1. **A reason to leave where you are** (dissatisfaction with your current situation)
2. **A vision of where you want to go** (a picture of something better)
3. **The courage to take the first step** (willingness to be uncomfortable)

Everything else—the knowledge, the connections, the money—comes after you start moving.

I didn't know how I was going to pay for college when I got on that bus. I didn't know if I was fast enough to compete at a higher level. I didn't even know where Garden City, Kansas was on a map.

But I knew I couldn't stay where I was.

Sometimes the most important decision you'll ever make is the decision to get uncomfortable. To leave the familiar for the unknown. To bet on yourself when nobody else will.

That's what that box represented—a bet on myself. And every real estate deal I've done since then, every credit application I've submitted, every property I've purchased with other people's money—it all traces back to the courage I found sitting on that Greyhound bus with everything I owned in a cardboard box.

The question isn't whether you have enough to start. The question is whether you have enough courage to start with what you have.

**Your box is waiting. Where's your bus headed?**

# CHAPTER 2

## Running Toward Freedom

The first thing that hit me when I stepped off that Greyhound bus in Garden City, Kansas wasn't the cold—though Lord knows it was colder than anything I'd experienced in East Texas. It was the silence.

I'm talking about a different kind of quiet than you've ever heard if you've lived in a city your whole life. This was the sound of absolutely nothing for miles in every direction. No traffic, no sirens, no neighbors arguing through thin walls. Just wind and space and the sudden realization that I was further from home than I'd ever been in my life.

Me and those three other guys from Texas looked around at each other like we'd made some kind of terrible mistake. One of them actually said what we were all thinking: "Bro, what have we done?"

But you know what? That silence became my sanctuary. Because for the first time in my life, the only voice I had to listen to was my own.

### The Middle of Nowhere University

Garden City Junior College wasn't much to look at. A few brick buildings spread across what used to be farmland, dormitories that looked like they were built in the 1960s and hadn't been updated since, and a track that was decent but nothing special.

What it did have was something I'd never experienced before: structure without chaos.

Back home in Longview, there was always something going on. Drama in the neighborhood, family stuff, friends getting into trouble, distractions everywhere. Here, there was nothing to do but focus on the two things that could get me out: running and studying.

The running program was legit. Coach Self had been there for many years and had sent dozens of guys to four-year schools. He was old school—demanding, disciplined, and he didn't care about your feelings. He cared about your times.

"Patterson," he told me on my first day, "I don't know what you did in Texas, but that's over now. Here, you run my workouts, you follow my schedule, and you get better, or you go home."

I respected that. I needed that.

### Learning the 10,000-Hour Rule the Hard Way

If you've never run cross country in Kansas, let me paint the picture for you. It's flat. So flat that you can see for miles in every direction, which sounds beautiful until you're three miles into a six-mile run and you can see exactly how much further you have to go.

The weather doesn't care about your training schedule. I ran in snow, sleet, rain, and heat that felt just as brutal as Texas but somehow different. Kansas heat is dry; it sucks the moisture right out of you. Texas heat is humid; it wraps around you like a wet blanket. Both will test your mental toughness.

But here's what I learned about running that changed everything about how I approach challenges: **it's all in your control.**

In basketball, you need your teammates to set screens, pass you the ball, play defense. You need the ref to make fair calls. You need the coach to draw up plays that work. But running? Running is just you against you. Your effort, your discipline, your mental toughness.

If you put in the work, you get better. If you slack off, your times show it. If you're consistent, you improve. If you quit, you fail. It's the purest form of accountability I've ever experienced.

This was my introduction to the 10,000-hour rule, even though I didn't know what to call it at the time. Malcolm Gladwell talks about how it takes roughly 10,000 hours of deliberate practice to become world-class at anything. I wasn't trying to become world-class at running—I was trying to become good enough to get a scholarship to a better school.

But the principle was the same: consistent effort over time creates exponential results.

Every day, I was putting in 2-3 hours of training. Running, weights, stretching, studying film of my form. Over two years, that added up to over 1,500 hours of deliberate practice. And my times dropped significantly.

More importantly, I was learning that I could get good at something through pure effort and consistency, even if I didn't start with natural talent.

## The Exposure That Changes Everything

The thing about junior college athletics is that it's all about what comes next. Every meet, every race, every workout is really an audition for the next level. Coaches from four-year schools would come to our meets, stopwatches in hand, looking for diamonds in the rough.

I started meeting guys who had already made the transition. Dudes who had come from similar backgrounds—small towns, limited resources, big dreams—and had used junior college as a stepping stone to places like Arkansas, Oklahoma, Nebraska, Georgia.

These conversations were my real education. Not just about running, but about possibility.

"Man," one guy told me, "you don't even know what's out there. These big schools have facilities you can't imagine. Academic support. Tutoring. Resources. And if you're good enough, they'll take care of everything."

Everything? I could barely imagine what "everything" looked like.

But the more I heard, the more I wanted it. And the more I wanted it, the harder I trained.

## The Grade Reality Check

Here's what they don't tell you about being a student-athlete: you're a student first, athlete second, whether you like it or not. And I was learning that the hard way.

My grades in high school had been mediocre at best. I was passing, but just barely. I thought college would be different because I was more motivated, but motivation doesn't automatically translate to study skills.

I was failing my first semester. Not just struggling—failing.

My coach pulled me aside after about six weeks and laid it out straight: "Patterson, I don't care how fast you run. If you don't get your grades right, you're going home. And not just home for the semester—home forever. No four-year school is going to touch you with bad grades."

That was my wake-up call.

I had to learn how to study. Actually study, not just read the same page five times and hope something stuck. I had to learn how to take notes, how to manage my time, how to ask for help when I didn't understand something.

The same discipline I was applying to running, I started applying to academics. I treated studying like training. Scheduled time, specific goals, measurable results.

By the end of that first semester, I was pulling C's and B's. By the end of my time at Garden City, I was consistently on the Dean's List.

**The Transfer Process**

Halfway through my second year, the phone calls started coming. Coaches from four-year schools who had seen my times, looked at my grades, and thought I might be a good fit for their programs.

Arkansas. Oklahoma. Nebraska. And Georgia.

My roommate, who was from a town right next to Longview, had been talking to the coach at Georgia. After he got off one of those calls, he looked at me and said, "Man, I'm going to Athens. You should come too."

Georgia? I'll be honest—I thought the University of Georgia was in Atlanta. I had visions of the big city, nightlife, culture, all the things you see in movies about college life.

"Where's Athens?" I asked him.

"About an hour from Atlanta," he said. "It's a college town."

A college town. That sounded perfect. Not too big, not too small. Close enough to a major city but not overwhelming.

I called the coach, sent my transcripts, and waited.

## The Visit That Opened My Eyes

When I finally made my official visit to Georgia, reality hit me in ways I wasn't prepared for. First, Athens wasn't Atlanta. It was about an hour and a half away, down a long road called University Parkway. I kept looking back at the Atlanta skyline in the distance slowly disappearing.

But Athens was beautiful in its own way. Rolling hills, historic buildings, and a campus that felt like what I imagined college was supposed to look like.

What really struck me, though, was the scale. The football stadium held 92,000 people. The track facility was better than anything I'd ever seen. The academic buildings looked like something out of a movie.

And then there were the people.

This was 1999, so we're talking about a different era in terms of racial dynamics in the South. I was one of maybe three black students I saw during my entire visit, and the only other black people I encountered were either athletes or working in food service and maintenance.

That was... eye-opening.

Coming from East Texas, I was used to being around people who looked like me. Garden City had been diverse in its own way—lots of different backgrounds brought together by athletics and academics. But Georgia felt different.

Not necessarily hostile, but definitely different.

**The Culture Shock of Success**

What really blew my mind wasn't the racial dynamics—it was the wealth dynamics. During my visit, it was rush week for the sororities. I'm watching hundreds of young women dressed to the nines, standing in front of these massive houses that looked like mansions, competing to get into organizations that their parents were paying thousands of dollars for them to join.

I'd never seen anything like it.

"What's all this?" I asked my host.

"Rush week," he said, like it was the most normal thing in the world. "Sorority girls trying to get into the houses they want."

Houses? These weren't houses. These were estates. With columns and manicured lawns and parking lots full of cars that cost more than my family's yearly income.

And these girls—they weren't just hoping to get in. They were competing. Begging, really. To pay money to be part of something.

That's when I realized I was in a different world. A world where people had so much money that they could afford to pay for friendships, for status, for experiences that I couldn't even imagine wanting because I'd never known they existed.

But instead of feeling intimidated, I felt motivated. If this level of wealth existed, if people my age were already living like this, then it meant wealth was possible. It meant that the American Dream wasn't just a story they told poor kids to keep them working hard—it was actually achievable.

I just had to figure out how.

## The Commitment

The running program at Georgia was exactly what I needed. High-level competition, excellent coaching, and the kind of resources that could take my performance to the next level.

But more than that, Georgia represented exposure. Exposure to different ways of thinking, different levels of wealth, different possibilities for what life could look like.

I committed on the spot.

"Coach," I told him, "I want to be here."

And just like that, the kid who had left East Texas with everything he owned in a cardboard box was heading to the University of Georgia on an athletic scholarship.

## The Real Education Begins

What I didn't realize at the time was that the real education wasn't going to happen in the classroom or on the track. It was going to happen in the spaces between—watching how people with money moved through the world, learning about systems and structures I'd never been exposed to, understanding that wealth wasn't just about having money but about having access.

Access to opportunities. Access to information. Access to networks that could change your entire life trajectory.

That box that had carried me from Longview to Garden City to Athens had been my classroom in resourcefulness. Now I was about to get a master class in possibility.

## House Money Hack: Seek Uncomfortable Growth

Here's what I learned during those two years in Kansas that applies directly to building wealth: **growth happens when you put yourself in situations that demand more from you than you've ever given before.**

Running 60+ miles a week in brutal weather conditions taught me that I could do hard things consistently. Managing a full course load while training taught me time management. Being away from everything familiar taught me self-reliance.

These weren't just life skills—they were wealth-building skills.

When I started investing in real estate years later, I wasn't intimidated by the complexity because I'd already proven to myself that I could master difficult things through consistent effort.

When I had to learn about credit scores and business funding, I wasn't overwhelmed because I'd already developed the discipline to study things I didn't naturally understand.

When I had to take risks on property deals, I wasn't paralyzed by fear because I'd already gotten comfortable being uncomfortable.

**The principle is simple: put yourself in environments that force you to level up.**

If you want to build wealth, you need to develop wealth-building muscles: discipline, delayed gratification, calculated risk-taking, continuous learning, and mental toughness.

The best way to develop these muscles is to put yourself in situations where you have no choice but to use them.

Maybe that's taking a job that scares you because it pays more but demands more. Maybe it's moving to a new city where you don't know anyone. Maybe it's starting a side business even though you've never been an entrepreneur.

Whatever it is, the principle is the same: **comfort is the enemy of growth.**

That bus to Kansas was uncomfortable. Those two years of grueling training and academic discipline were uncomfortable. Being one of the only black students on a predominantly white campus was uncomfortable.

But every uncomfortable situation prepared me for the next level of opportunity.

**Your running shoes are laced up. Where's your Kansas?**

# CHAPTER 3

## The American Dream Detour

W hen I stepped onto the University of Georgia campus in August 1997, I thought I had arrived. Full scholarship, Division I athletics, one of the best public universities in the South—this was everything I had dreamed about during those long runs in Kansas.

What I didn't realize was that I was about to get an education in more than just academics and athletics. I was about to learn about class, race, money, and power in ways that would fundamentally change how I saw the world.

**The Reality of Being "The Only"**

My first day of classes hit me like a cold slap of reality. I walked into my speech communication class—a lecture hall with about 200 students—and as I scanned the room looking for a seat, I realized something that made my stomach drop.

I was the only Black student in the entire class.

Not just one of a few. The *only* one.

I sat down in the back row and looked around again, thinking maybe I had missed someone. Nope. Two hundred white faces and me.

This wasn't like Garden City, where the diversity came from different states and backgrounds. This was the Deep South in the mid-90s, and the social dynamics were... complicated.

It wasn't that anyone was openly hostile. Most people were polite, even friendly. But there was this underlying awareness, this constant reminder that I was different, that I was being watched, that I represented more than just myself.

When the professor called on me, I could feel everyone turning to look. When I spoke up in class discussions, I could sense people evaluating not just what I said, but how I said it. When I walked across campus in my team gear, I could feel the weight of being not just a student-athlete, but a Black student-athlete at a predominantly white institution.

## The Service Economy Revelation

What really opened my eyes wasn't the classroom dynamics—it was everything happening outside the classroom.

The dining halls, the maintenance crews, the custodial staff, the groundskeepers—they were almost all Black. The professors, the administrators, the students, the sorority and fraternity members—they were almost all white.

I'm not saying this to be divisive or to complain. I'm stating facts about what I observed. And those facts taught me something crucial about how wealth and power work in America.

The people who looked like me were serving. The people who didn't look like me were being served.

Now, there's nothing wrong with honest work. My family had taught me that any job that puts food on the table is honorable work. But I also started to understand that there were different levels of the economic game, and where you ended up often had more to do with access and opportunity than it did with how hard you worked.

The woman who cleaned our dorm worked harder physically than most of the students I knew. But she was making minimum wage while they were preparing for careers in business, law, and medicine.

That wasn't a judgment on anyone's character. That was a lesson about systems.

## Football Saturdays and Economic Reality

If you've never experienced a Georgia football Saturday, you can't understand the scale. Ninety-two thousand people packed into Sanford Stadium, most of them wearing red and black, all of them passionate about their Bulldogs.

What struck me wasn't just the size of the crowd—it was the economics of it all.

People were spending hundreds, sometimes thousands of dollars just for the weekend. Hotel rooms, restaurant meals, tickets, merchandise, tailgating supplies. I watched families drop more money on a single football weekend than my family spent on groceries in two months.

And sitting in those premium seats, walking through those VIP tailgate areas, driving those expensive cars—they were almost exclusively white.

Meanwhile, the team they were cheering for? The team that generated all this economic activity? We were almost exclusively Black.

Again, I'm not making judgments here. I'm making observations. And what I observed was that there were different ways to participate in the economy. You could be the entertainment, or you could be the audience. You could be the labor, or you could be the capital.

I decided I wanted to be the capital.

### The Academic Hustle

My major was speech communication, which sounds more impressive than it actually was. If I'm being honest, I chose it because it seemed manageable alongside my athletic commitments.

I wasn't trying to be a brain surgeon or a rocket scientist. I was trying to stay eligible to run track while figuring out what came next. My priority was athletics, and academics was just what I had to do to keep running.

But even with a relatively easy major, college was challenging. The reading load was heavy, the writing requirements were demanding, and the expectations were higher than anything I'd experienced.

I developed a system: I treated studying like training. Scheduled time blocks, specific goals, measurable outcomes. If I had a two-hour training session, I'd follow it with a two-hour study session. Same discipline, same commitment, same refusal to quit when it got difficult.

By my junior year, I was pulling A's and B's consistently. Not because I was naturally gifted academically, but because I had learned how to work smart and stay disciplined.

## Track Success and Professional Dreams

The running was going well. Better than well, actually. My times were dropping, I was competing at the SEC level, and for a brief period, I thought maybe—just maybe—I could make a career out of running professionally.

But reality has a way of humbling you.

I was fast, but I wasn't *that* fast. I was competitive at the college level, but the gap between college competitive and professional competitive is massive. I could see it in the times, feel it in the workouts, know it in my heart.

I was going to need a backup plan.

## The Post-College Reality Check

When I graduated in 2002, I did what most college graduates do: I tried to get a job in my field. Speech communication. Which, it turns out, isn't really a field so much as it's a major.

I sent out resumes, went on interviews, and quickly learned that a college degree—even from a good school like Georgia—doesn't automatically translate to a good job, especially when you don't have connections or family wealth to fall back on.

I ended up working at a physical therapy clinic, initially as a technician working under a doctor's license. The pay was decent—better than anything I'd ever made—and the work was satisfying. I was helping people recover from injuries, getting them back to their normal lives.

More importantly, it was stable. Regular hours, steady paycheck, health insurance, the whole package.

For the first time in my life, I could afford to buy things I wanted instead of just things I needed. I got my first nice car—not luxury, but reliable and presentable. I bought my first house—a small place, but it was *mine*.

I was living the American Dream, right? College degree, steady job, house, car, savings account. This was what I had been working toward since that day I got on the Greyhound bus in Texas.

So why did it feel like something was missing?

## The Restlessness

About two years into the physical therapy job, I started feeling restless. Not unhappy, exactly, but unsatisfied. Like I was playing it safe when I should be taking risks. Like I was settling when I should be reaching.

I remember patients and coworkers telling me, "Man, you're young, you're smart, you could do anything. Why are you here?"

It wasn't that they were putting down the job—it was good work with good people. But they saw something in me that I was starting to see in myself: potential that wasn't being fully utilized.

I started having this recurring thought: *Your calling is going to keep calling you until you answer.*

I didn't know what that calling was yet, but I knew it wasn't physical therapy.

## The Food Business Opportunity

That's when I met Coach Ray Goff, the former UGA football coach. Through a mutual connection, I ended up having dinner with him and another guy—a Black administrator at the university who had money to invest.

Coach Goff had been involved in some Zaxby's franchise opportunities and was looking for partners who could help him manage and grow stores. Specifically, he was looking for people who could connect with the community, work hard, and learn the business.

"Look," he told us over dinner, "this has been lucrative for me. I'm telling y'all what y'all need to do, because I see potential in both of you."

The opportunity was this: they had identified some underperforming Zaxby's locations in Arkansas. Stores that were already operational but not meeting their potential. We could buy them out, turn them around, and build a regional presence.

I would be the boots-on-the-ground guy. The other investor would provide the capital and business oversight. Coach Goff would provide the connections and industry knowledge.

It meant leaving my stable job, leaving Georgia, and moving to Arkansas for at least six months. It meant taking a risk on an industry I knew nothing about, with partners I barely knew, in a state I'd never lived in.

But it also meant ownership. Equity. The possibility of building something instead of just working for someone else.

## The Arkansas Experiment

I took the leap.

I gave my notice at the physical therapy clinic, packed up my life (which thankfully didn't require as many boxes as it had when I left Texas), and drove to Arkansas.

For six months, I lived in a hotel. Every single day, I was in those restaurants—learning the operations, training staff, implementing new systems, figuring out why these stores weren't performing and how to fix them.

The work was intense. Restaurant management is no joke—you're dealing with inventory, staffing, customer service, food quality, health department regulations, and profit margins all at the same time. And you're doing it 12-14 hours a day, six days a week.

But I was learning. Not just about the restaurant business, but about business in general. How to read financial statements. How to manage people. How to solve problems quickly. How to make decisions with incomplete information.

And the money was good. Better than good. I was earning more in six months than I had made in two years at the physical therapy clinic.

**The Lifestyle Reality Check**

Here's what they don't tell you about making good money in a demanding business: sometimes the cost is higher than the paycheck.

I was making more money than I'd ever made, but I had no time to enjoy it. I was working so much that my health was suffering—no time for exercise, eating restaurant food constantly, stressed about operations and staff and numbers.

I had no personal life. No time for relationships, hobbies, travel, or any of the things that make life worth living.

Essentially, I had traded time and health for money. And while the money was good, the trade-off didn't feel sustainable.

More importantly, I started to realize that even though I had ownership in these stores, I wasn't really building wealth—I was just buying myself a high-paying job.

**The Pivot Point**

After about a year in Arkansas and Georgia, I made a decision that surprised everyone, including myself: I was going to leave the restaurant business.

Not because it wasn't profitable—it was. Not because I couldn't handle the work—I could. But because I could see that this path, successful as it might be, wasn't leading me where I wanted to go.

I wanted freedom. Time freedom. Location freedom. The ability to make money without trading every hour of my life for it.

The restaurant business, no matter how profitable, was still essentially trading time for money. And I was starting to understand that real wealth comes from assets that work for you, not jobs that work you to death.

## The Real Estate Revelation

What I had learned from the Zaxby's experience was something that would change my entire approach to wealth building: the real money wasn't in the chicken.

It was in the dirt the chicken was sitting on.

We had set up two separate LLCs—one for the restaurant operations and one for the real estate. The restaurant LLC paid rent to the real estate LLC. The idea was that once the restaurant operations paid off the property, we'd own the real estate free and clear, creating two income streams: the business and the rent.

That was my first real introduction to the concept of real estate as an investment vehicle. And it planted a seed that would eventually grow into my entire wealth-building strategy.

But first, I had to get back to Athens, Georgia and figure out my next move.

## House Money Hack: Distinguish Between Income and Wealth

The biggest lesson from my restaurant experience was understanding the difference between making money and building wealth. This distinction is crucial for anyone trying to create financial freedom.

**Income** is money you earn from working. It stops when you stop working. Even if it's good income—like what I was making from the restaurants—it's still fundamentally tied to your time and effort.

**Wealth** is money that works for you. Assets that generate income whether you're actively involved or not. Real estate, business ownership, investments that compound over time.

The restaurant business was generating good income, but it wasn't building wealth. I was still trading my time for money, just at a higher hourly rate.

Real wealth comes from systems and assets that can operate independently of your daily involvement. That's what creates true freedom—the ability to earn money while you sleep, travel, or pursue other interests.

When evaluating any opportunity, ask yourself: "Am I buying a job or building an asset?"

Jobs, no matter how well-paying, keep you trapped in the cycle of trading time for money. Assets free you from that cycle by generating passive income.

**The most expensive money you'll ever make is money that costs you your freedom.**

Understanding this distinction changed how I evaluated every opportunity that came after Arkansas. Instead of asking, "How much can I make?" I started asking, "How can this help me build wealth?"

That shift in thinking set the stage for everything that came next.

**Your American Dream might be someone else's nightmare. What does freedom actually look like to you?**

# PART II:
# THE AWAKENING

# CHAPTER 4

# The Running Partner's Wisdom

When I came back to Athens from Arkansas, I felt like I was starting over again. I was 35 years old, had some money saved from the restaurant business, but no clear direction on what came next. The physical therapy job was gone. The restaurant opportunity was behind me. I was essentially unemployed with a college degree and a head full of questions about what I actually wanted to do with my life.

But I still had my house in Athens. That little place I'd bought during my physical therapy days was still there, still mine, still representing the only piece of the American Dream I'd managed to hold onto.

And I still had my legs.

**Back to the Track**

One of the first things I did when I got back to town was head to the University of Georgia track. Not as a student-athlete anymore, but as an alum who needed to clear his head and figure out his next move.

Running has always been my form of therapy. When life gets complicated, when decisions need to be made, when I need to think clearly—I run. There's something about the rhythm of your feet hitting the ground, the steady breathing, the meditative quality of forward motion that helps everything else fall into place.

I wasn't the only one with this idea.

The track at UGA attracts all kinds of people—current students, former athletes, community members who just want access to a quality facility. After a few days of running solo, I started noticing the same faces, the same routines, the same people who were out there consistently.

One of those faces belonged to Mike Swoopes, a former teammate. He'd been a few years ahead of me, also ran track, but we'd never really connected during our competitive years.

Now we were both post-college adults, both clearly using the track for more than just fitness, both running at a pace that suggested we had time to talk.

## The Six-Mile MBA

"You want to start meeting up four to five times a week to run?" Mike asked one afternoon as I was warming up.

"Sure, man. I could use the company."

What started as casual conversation during an easy six-mile run turned into the most valuable education I've ever received. Because Mike wasn't just running for exercise—he was running a real estate business.

As we settled into our pace, he started telling me about his day. Not in a bragging way, but just casual conversation about what he'd been working on. Looking at properties. Meeting with contractors. Dealing with tenants. Collecting rent checks.

"Wait," I said about two miles in, "you own rental properties?"

"Yeah, man. I got into it a few years ago. College housing, mostly. Buy houses near campus, rent them out by the room to students."

By the room? That was a concept I'd never heard of or thought much about.

"Instead of renting a whole house to one family for, say, $1,200 a month, I rent each bedroom to a different student for $400 each. Four bedrooms, $1,600 total. Same house, more income."

The math was simple, but the implications were huge. This wasn't just about real estate—this was about thinking creatively, finding angles that other people missed, maximizing the value of assets you already owned.

**The Daily Classroom**

What started as one conversation turned into a daily routine. Every morning, Marcus and I would meet at the track for our six or seven-mile run. And every day, for 45-50 minutes, I was getting a master class in real estate investing.

He told me about his first deal—a small house he'd bought near campus, how nervous he'd been, how he'd almost talked himself out of it. He told me about his mistakes—tenants who'd trashed places, repairs that cost more than expected, deals that looked good on paper but fell apart in reality.

But he also told me about his successes. Properties that had doubled in value. Rent checks that came in like clockwork. The freedom of having income that wasn't directly tied to trading his time for money.

"Man," he said during one particularly long run, "I used to think real estate was for rich people. Like you needed huge down payments and perfect credit and all this knowledge I didn't have. But once I got started, I realized it's really just about understanding the numbers and being willing to learn as you go."

I was asking questions constantly. How did he find properties? How did he know what to pay? How did he screen tenants? How did he handle repairs? How did he finance everything?

Mike answered every single question, generously and thoroughly. He never acted like I was bothering him or taking up his time. He seemed genuinely excited to share what he'd learned.

"Look," he told me one day, "I learned this stuff by making mistakes and figuring it out as I went. If I can help you avoid some of those mistakes and get started faster, that's good for both of us. More people succeeding in real estate just makes the whole market better."

### The Athens Advantage

What Mike helped me understand was that Athens, Georgia was actually a perfect place to get started in real estate. It had all the advantages of a college town with none of the disadvantages of a big city.

College towns have built-in demand. Students need housing every semester, and they're willing to pay premium rents for convenience and nice amenities. Parents are often willing to pay higher rents if it means their kids are living somewhere safe and well-maintained.

Athens specifically had some unique advantages:

**Small town prices, city town rents.** Because Athens was an hour from Atlanta, property prices were reasonable compared to big metropolitan areas. But because it was home to the University of Georgia—a major state university—rent demand was strong and consistent.

**Stable population.** Every semester brought new students who needed housing. Every year brought new freshman classes. The population might fluctuate seasonally, but the demand for housing was predictable.

**Limited supply.** The university kept growing, but the amount of land near campus was fixed. Basic supply and demand economics suggested that property values and rents would continue to increase over time.

Mike was buying houses within walking distance of campus, fixing them up to appeal to college students, and renting them by the room. He was averaging about 15-20% cash returns on his investments, which was significantly better than anything he could get from stocks, bonds, or savings accounts.

**The Niche Discovery**

"You know what's interesting?" Mike said during one of our runs. "You keep asking me about different types of real estate—commercial, multi-family, fix-and-flip. But I think you've already found your niche. You just don't realize it yet."

"What do you mean?"

"Man, you know this market better than most people ever will. You lived here as a student. You understand what students want, what they're willing to pay for, what problems they have with housing. You know the neighborhoods, the campus, the culture. That's not knowledge you can get from books—that's insider information."

He was right. I did know Athens from the student perspective. I knew which areas were most convenient, which neighborhoods felt safe, what amenities mattered most to college students.

"Plus," he continued, "you're young enough to relate to the tenants, old enough to be taken seriously as a landlord, and you've got the work ethic to handle the management side. That's a rare combination."

I started to see what he meant. Instead of trying to compete with experienced investors in markets I didn't understand, I could leverage my existing knowledge and connections in a market I knew intimately.

**The Learning Process**

Over about six months of these daily runs, Marcus basically gave me a complete education in real estate investing. But he did more than just share information—he showed me how to think about it.

He taught me to evaluate properties based on numbers, not emotions. "You're not buying a home," he'd say. "You're buying a business. The only question that matters is: will this business be profitable?"

He taught me to think long-term. "Real estate isn't a get-rich-quick scheme. It's a get-rich-slow plan. You make money through cash flow, appreciation, and tax benefits over time."

He taught me to start small and scale gradually. "Don't try to buy a 20-unit apartment building on your first deal. Buy one house, learn the process, make your mistakes on a small scale, then use what you learn to do bigger deals."

Most importantly, he taught me that real estate investing wasn't about having perfect knowledge or unlimited capital—it was about taking action with the resources you had and learning as you went.

## The Encouragement I Needed

About eight months into our running partnership, I finally worked up the courage to tell Mike what I was really thinking: "Man, I want to do what you're doing. I want to get into real estate."

"I've been wondering when you were going to say that," he laughed. "You've been asking real estate questions for months. I figured you were either planning to compete with me or partner with me."

"Actually," I said, "I was hoping you might teach me how to get started."

"Bro, I've been teaching you for eight months. You already know everything you need to know to buy your first property. The only thing stopping you now is fear."

He was right. I had the knowledge. I had some money saved from the restaurant business. I had a stable living situation and good credit. What I didn't have was the confidence to pull the trigger.

"Look," Mike said, "I'll make you a deal. When you find your first property, I'll look at the numbers with you. If it's a good deal, I'll encourage you to move forward. If it's not, I'll tell you to walk away. But you have to actually start looking."

That was exactly the safety net I needed. Someone with experience who could help me avoid making a huge mistake on my first deal.

"And one more thing," he added. "I don't think you should try to do exactly what I'm doing. College housing is way more numbers, risk and money. But single-family homes? Regular rental properties? There's plenty of opportunity there. You should focus on that market."

## The Mentorship Model

Looking back, what Marcus gave me was more than just real estate education—he gave me a model for how mentorship should work.

He didn't charge me for his time or try to sell me a course. He didn't gate-keep information or make me feel like I was competing with him. He didn't overwhelm me with complex strategies or advanced techniques.

Instead, he met me where I was, answered the questions I was actually asking, and gradually built my confidence and knowledge over time. He made himself available consistently but let me drive the conversation based on my interests and readiness to learn.

Most importantly, he encouraged me to adapt his strategies to my own situation rather than trying to copy exactly what he was doing.

That model of mentorship—generous, gradual, and tailored to the individual—became the template for how I try to teach others today.

**House Money Hack: Find Your Daily Mentor**

The most valuable education I ever received happened during 45-minute runs, six days a week, over eight months. Not in a classroom, not in a seminar, not in an expensive mastermind program—just in daily conversations with someone who was already doing what I wanted to do.

Here's how to create your own "running partner" mentorship:

**1. Identify someone who's already successful in your area of interest.** Look for people who are a few steps ahead of you, not decades ahead. You want someone whose success feels achievable, not impossibly distant.

**2. Find a natural reason to spend regular time together.** Maybe it's exercise, maybe it's volunteering, maybe it's a hobby you both enjoy. The key is consistency and low pressure—not formal "pick your brain" meetings.

**3. Ask specific, actionable questions.** Instead of "How do I get started in real estate?" ask "How do you analyze whether a property will cash flow positive?" Specific questions get specific answers.

**4. Implement what you learn and report back.** The best way to keep someone engaged in mentoring you is to show that you're taking action on their advice. People love to help people who help themselves.

**5. Add value in return.** Even if you're the student, find ways to be useful to your mentor. Maybe you have skills they need, connections they want, or simply enthusiasm that reminds them why they love their business.

**6. Be patient and consistent.** Real mentorship happens over months and years, not days and weeks. Trust the process of gradual learning and relationship building.

The goal isn't to find someone who will give you all the answers—it's to find someone who will help you discover the right questions and guide you toward finding your own answers.

**Marcus didn't just teach me about real estate. He taught me how to think like an investor. That mindset shift was worth more than any specific technique or strategy.**

**Your mentor might be running circles around the track right now. Are you ready to lace up your shoes?**

# CHAPTER 5

## Credit Confessions

The phone call that changed my life came on a Tuesday afternoon in 2018. I was sitting in my little house in Athens, scrolling through real estate listings online, doing what I'd been doing for months—looking at properties I couldn't afford to buy.

I had the knowledge. Thanks to Mike and our daily runs, I understood how to analyze deals, what to look for in properties, how rental income worked, and what constituted a good investment. I had some money saved from my restaurant days—enough for maybe one small down payment if I found the right deal.

What I didn't have was enough money to scale. In real estate, the 20-25% down payment requirement means you run out of cash fast. Buy one property, and you're tapped out until you save up another down payment, which could take years.

I was stuck in what I call the "one-and-done" trap. I could afford to be a real estate investor, but not a real estate business owner.

That's when the phone rang.

## The Mentor I Didn't Know I Needed

"Lee, this is David Mitchell. We haven't met, but I got your name from Mike Swope. He said you're interested in real estate but might need some help with the financing side."

David was a guy Mike had met at a real estate investing meetup. He'd been in the business for about ten years, but his specialty wasn't just buying properties—it was teaching people how to fund their real estate investments using business credit and alternative financing methods.

"Miike tells me you're smart, motivated, and understand the real estate side, but you're running into the same problem everybody runs into—you need more capital to scale."

He was right. That was exactly my problem.

"What if I told you there was a way to access funding for real estate that didn't require you to use your own money, didn't require traditional bank financing, and didn't require you to wait years between deals?"

I'll be honest—my first thought was that this sounded too good to be true. But Mike had recommended him, and Mike hadn't steered me wrong yet.

"I'm listening," I said.

## The Credit Reality Check

"Before we talk about solutions," David said, "let me ask you some questions about your current financial situation. What's your credit score?"

I knew this question was coming, but I still wasn't prepared for how embarrassing it was to answer.

"It's... not great. Probably around 680, maybe 690."

There was a pause on the other end of the line.

"Okay, when's the last time you pulled your actual credit report and looked at what's on there?"

"Honestly? I haven't looked at it in probably two years. I know there are some issues from college—credit cards I got behind on, a cell phone bill that went to collections, probably some other stuff."

"Lee, I'm going to say this with respect, but you can't manage what you don't measure. If you're serious about real estate investing, you're going to need to get serious about understanding and improving your credit. Because credit is the foundation of everything we're going to talk about."

That was my first wake-up call. I'd been thinking about credit as this abstract number that was either good or bad, not as something I could actively manage and improve.

"Here's what I want you to do," David continued. "Get a copy of your credit report from all three bureaus—Experian, Equifax, and TransUnion. Actually read through everything that's on there. Make a list of every negative item, every account that's behind, every collection that's outstanding. Then call me back, and we'll talk about how to fix it."

## The Credit Report Horror Show

When I finally pulled my credit reports, it was worse than I'd imagined. Not just bad—catastrophically bad.

There were credit cards I'd forgotten about from college that had gone into default. A gym membership that had apparently continued charging me after I moved. That cell phone bill I mentioned. A medical bill from an emergency room visit that I thought my insurance had covered but apparently hadn't.

My credit utilization was terrible—I had a few cards that were maxed out or close to it. My payment history was inconsistent. I had no recent positive credit history because I'd basically been avoiding credit altogether for the past few years.

Looking at those reports was like getting a full-body scan and discovering you had problems in places you didn't even know existed.

But David had prepared me for this. "Don't get overwhelmed," he'd said. "Bad credit is just a problem to be solved, not a permanent condition. Everything on your credit report can be fixed, removed, or improved. It's just a matter of knowing the process and being disciplined about following it."

## The Five-Factor Education

When I called David back with my credit report summary, he launched into what he called "Credit 101"—the five factors that determine your credit score and how to optimize each one.

"**Payment History** is 35% of your score," he explained. "This is the big one. Going forward, you need to pay everything on time, every time. No exceptions. Set up automatic payments if you have to, but never miss another payment."

"**Credit Utilization** is 30% of your score. This is how much of your available credit you're using. You want to keep this below 30%, ideally below 10%. If you have a $1,000 credit limit, you don't want to carry more than $100-300 in debt."

"**Length of Credit History** is 15% of your score. You can't change how long you've had credit, but you can avoid closing old accounts, which would shorten your average account age."

"**Credit Mix** is 10% of your score. Having different types of credit—credit cards, installment loans, maybe a car loan—shows you can manage various types of debt responsibly."

"**New Credit** is 10% of your score. This is about how often you apply for new credit. Too many applications in a short time period makes you look desperate and hurts your score."

"The good news," David said, "is that most of this is under your control. You can't change your past payment history, but you can control every payment going forward. You can't instantly fix your credit mix, but you can optimize your utilization immediately."

## The Dispute Process

David then walked me through the process of disputing negative items on my credit report. This was something I'd never known was possible—I thought once something was on your credit report, it was there forever.

"The credit reporting system is far from perfect," he explained. "Mistakes happen all the time. Accounts get reported to the wrong person, dates get entered incorrectly, debts that have been paid off show as still outstanding. You have the right to dispute anything on your credit report that's inaccurate, and the credit bureaus have to investigate."

He taught me how to write dispute letters, what documentation to include, how to follow up, and what to do if my disputes were denied.

More importantly, he taught me that even legitimate negative items could sometimes be removed through negotiation with creditors. "If you owe money and you're willing to pay it," he said, "many creditors will agree to remove the negative reporting in exchange for payment. It's called a 'pay for delete' agreement."

## The 90-Day Transformation

David gave me a 90-day action plan to improve my credit score:

### Days 1-30: Damage Control

- Pull all three credit reports and create a master list of issues
- Contact every creditor with outstanding balances and negotiate payment plans
- Pay down credit card balances to below 30% utilization

- Set up automatic payments for all current accounts

## Days 31-60: Active Improvement

- Submit dispute letters for any inaccurate information
- Negotiate pay-for-delete agreements with collection agencies
- Pay down credit card balances to below 10% utilization
- Apply for one new credit card to improve credit mix (if qualified)

## Days 61-90: Fine-Tuning

- Follow up on all disputes
- Continue paying down balances
- Monitor credit score improvements
- Begin researching business credit establishment

"The goal," David said, "isn't to get perfect credit overnight. The goal is to get your credit good enough that you can start accessing business funding. For what we're going to do, you need to get to at least 650 personal credit, ideally 700+."

## The Business Credit Revelation

Once we had a plan for fixing my personal credit, David introduced me to a concept I'd never heard of: business credit.

"Personal credit is what most people know about," he explained. "It's tied to your Social Security number, it's based on your personal financial history, and it's what banks look at when you apply for a car loan or mortgage."

"Business credit is completely separate. It's tied to your business's EIN (Employer Identification Number), it's based on your business's financial history, and it opens up a whole different world of funding opportunities."

The key insight was that business credit was evaluated differently than personal credit. While personal credit was mostly about your history as an individual borrower, business credit was about your business's potential for profitability and growth.

"Here's the beautiful thing about business credit," David said. "You can get approved for significant amounts of funding—$10,000, $50,000, $100,000 or more—without providing tax returns, bank statements, or personal financial statements. They're evaluating your business's creditworthiness, not your personal creditworthiness."

### The Setup Process

David walked me through the process of setting up a business entity that could build business credit:

**Step 1: Form a Legal Business Entity** I needed to set up an LLC or corporation that was properly registered with the state, had its own EIN from the IRS, and was set up to conduct real estate investment business.

**Step 2: Establish Business Banking** The business needed its own bank account, separate from my personal accounts, with some business activity flowing through it.

**Step 3: Get a Business Phone Number and Address** The business needed a dedicated phone line and a professional address (not "Grandma's house," as David put it). These details mattered for how creditors perceived the legitimacy of the business.

**Step 4: Build Business Credit References** Start with vendors and suppliers that report to business credit bureaus—phone companies, office supply stores, equipment leasing companies. Make small purchases, pay on time, and build a positive payment history.

**Step 5: Apply for Business Credit Cards and Lines of Credit** Once the foundation was established, begin applying for business credit products that reported to business credit bureaus.

### The Timeline Reality

"How long does this take?" I asked.

"To set up the business properly? About 30 days. To build enough business credit history to access significant funding? About 6-12 months if you do everything right."

That felt like forever when I was eager to start buying properties immediately. But David put it in perspective:

"Lee, you're 26 years old. You've got 40+ years of wealth-building ahead of you. Spending one year to set up a funding system that can support decades of real estate investing is the best investment you'll ever make."

He was right. I was thinking short-term when I needed to be thinking long-term.

## The First Application

Three months later, after following David's credit repair plan religiously, my personal credit score had improved from 580 to 670. Not perfect, but a dramatic improvement.

My business entity was set up correctly, I had established some business credit references, and David said I was ready to make my first business credit application.

"We're going to start small," he said. "Apply for a business credit card with a $5,000 limit. Use it for business expenses, pay it off every month, and establish a positive payment history."

I was approved.

When I got that first business credit card in the mail, it felt like I was holding a key to a door I didn't even know existed. Not because of the $5,000 credit limit—that wasn't going to buy me a house. But because it proved that the system David had taught me actually worked.

If I could get approved for $5,000 with limited business credit history, what could I get approved for with six months of perfect payment history? A year? Two years?

## House Money Hack: Credit is a Skill, Not a Gift

The biggest revelation from my credit education was understanding that credit isn't something you either have or don't have—it's something you build systematically over time.

Most people think about credit passively. They check their score occasionally, hope it's good enough for whatever they need, and accept whatever number they see as if it's permanent.

But credit is actually a skill you can develop, just like any other skill. There are specific actions that improve it, specific behaviors that hurt it, and specific strategies for optimizing it for your goals.

**Here's the system I learned:**

**1. Know Your Numbers** Pull your credit reports every 90 days. You can't improve what you don't measure. Many banks and credit card companies now provide free credit score monitoring.

**2. Optimize the Big Factors** Focus on payment history (35%) and credit utilization (30%) first. These have the biggest impact and are completely under your control.

**3. Think Business, Not Just Personal** Establish business credit parallel to personal credit. This doubles your funding capacity and creates opportunities that personal credit alone can't provide.

**4. Use Credit to Build Credit** Once you have access to credit, use it strategically to build more credit. Small balances paid off consistently build stronger credit than no activity at all.

**5. Plan Your Applications** Don't apply for credit randomly. Plan your applications around your goals—whether that's real estate investing, business funding, or major purchases.

**Business credit was the game-changer because it separated my personal financial capacity from my business financial capacity.**

Even if my personal credit was perfect, I'd still be limited by my personal income and assets. But business credit was evaluated based on business potential, not personal history.

That distinction opened up funding possibilities I never could have accessed through personal credit alone.

**Your credit score isn't your destiny—it's your starting point. Where are you going to take it?**

# CHAPTER 6

# First Flip, First Check

Nine months after my first conversation with David about credit repair, I was finally ready. My personal credit had climbed from 680 to 795. I had a properly established LLC with business banking and a clean business credit profile. I had $15,000 saved from my restaurant days, and access to about $75,000 in business credit across three different cards.

But there's a difference between being ready on paper and being ready in real life. I'd been analyzing deals for months, running numbers on properties, driving by potential investments. But I hadn't pulled the trigger on anything because I was terrified of making a mistake.

That's when the universe decided to force my hand.

**The Flyer That Changed Everything**

I was checking my mail on a Thursday afternoon when I found a yellow flyer stuck in my mailbox. The kind of thing I would normally throw away without reading. But something about the handwritten note at the bottom caught my eye:

*"Ready to sell? Cash buyer. Call Jennifer."*

The flyer was from a real estate agent named Jennifer Walsh. She was marketing to homeowners who might be interested in selling quickly for cash. What she probably didn't expect was to hear from someone who was looking to buy, not sell.

But I figured, why not? Maybe she knew about deals that weren't on the regular market yet.

I called the number.

"Hi, this is Lee Patterson. I got your flyer in my mailbox, but I'm actually on the other side—I'm looking to buy investment properties. Do you ever work with investors?"

"Actually, yes," Jennifer said. "I've got a property right now that might be perfect for an investor. The owner needs to sell quickly, and it's priced below market because of the timeline."

My heart started beating faster. This was it—my first real opportunity.

"Tell me about it," I said.

## The House on Broad Street

The property was a small single-family house on Broad Street, about five minutes from the UGA campus. Three bedrooms, one bathroom, about 1,100 square feet. Built in the 1950s but well-maintained.

The owner was an elderly woman who had inherited the house from her parents and used it as a rental for the past few years. But she was moving to Florida to be closer to her daughter and needed to sell quickly to close on her new place.

"She's asking $105,000," Jennifer told me. "But she's motivated. She might take less for a quick closing."

I grabbed a notepad and started running numbers while we talked:

- Purchase price: $105,000
- Estimated repairs needed: $5,000-$8,000 (mostly cosmetic)
- After-repair value: $125,000-$130,000
- Potential rental income: $950-$1,000 per month

Even at the asking price, this looked like it could work. If I could get it for less, it would be a solid first deal.

"Can I see it?" I asked.

We scheduled a showing for the next day.

## The Walk-Through

Meeting Jennifer at the property was my first real test of everything I'd learned from Marcus during our runs. I had to evaluate the house not as a potential home, but as a business investment.

The bones of the house were solid. Good foundation, roof looked decent, HVAC system was newer. The layout was functional for either a family rental or student housing—three bedrooms were enough to generate good rental income, and the location was convenient to campus.

The cosmetic issues were obvious but fixable: outdated paint through-out, carpet that needed to be replaced, kitchen appliances that were old but functional, bathrooms that needed updating.

I walked through each room, taking notes on my phone, mentally calculating repair costs based on conversations I'd had with contractors Mike had introduced me to.

"What do you think?" Jennifer asked as we finished the walk-through.

"I think it has potential," I said, trying to sound more confident than I felt. "But I'd need to come in under asking price to make the numbers work."

"What were you thinking?"

This was the moment of truth. I'd never negotiated a real estate deal before. I didn't know the local market well enough to know what constituted a reasonable offer. But I remembered something Mike had told me: "In real estate, you make your money when you buy, not when you sell. Don't be afraid to make offers that work for your numbers."

"I could do $95,000," I said.

Jennifer nodded. "Let me talk to the seller and see what she says."

**The Longest 48 Hours**

Waiting for a response on my first offer was agony. I kept running the numbers over and over, wondering if I'd offered too little, if I'd blown my first opportunity, if I should have offered more.

I called Mike to get his opinion.

"Man, relax," he said. "You made a reasonable offer based on your analysis. Either she accepts it, counters it, or rejects it. If she rejects it, there will be other deals. The worst thing you can do is chase a bad deal just because it's your first deal."

Friday afternoon, Jennifer called.

"She countered at $98,000," she said. "Cash closing in two weeks if possible."

I did quick math in my head. At $98,000, plus about $6,000 in repairs, I'd be all-in for $104,000. The house should rent for $1100-$1,500, and would probably be worth $125,000+ after repairs.

The numbers worked.

"I'll take it," I said.

## The Funding Strategy

Now came the real test of everything David had taught me about credit and funding. I had $15,000 in cash saved, but I needed about $25,000 total for the down payment (20% of $98,000 = $19,600) plus closing costs and repair money.

This is where business credit became crucial.

I applied for a 0% introductory APR business credit card with a $15,000 limit. The plan was to use this for the additional $10,000 I needed, then pay it off over the 12-month promotional period using rental income from the property.

The application was approved within 24 hours.

Between my saved cash and the business credit card, I had enough to close on the property and fund the necessary repairs.

## The Closing

Two weeks later, I was sitting in a title company office, signing more papers than I'd ever signed in my life. Purchase agreement, loan documents, title insurance, property disclosures—stack after stack of legal documents that would transfer ownership of real property from one person to another.

When the closing agent handed me the keys, I just stared at them for a moment.

I owned a house. Not the house I lived in—I'd bought that for personal use. This was different. This was a business asset. A property I'd bought specifically to generate income and build wealth.

It felt surreal.

## The Renovation

The next two weeks were a crash course in property management. I was coordinating painters, carpet installers, appliance deliveries, and utility transfers. I was learning about permits, inspections, and contractor scheduling.

Mike had given me a list of reliable contractors he'd worked with, which saved me from having to figure out who to trust with my investment. But I was still learning how to manage the process, how to ensure quality work, how to stay on budget and on schedule.

The total renovation ended up costing $6,500—within my estimated range. Fresh paint throughout, new carpet in all bedrooms, updated light fixtures, deep cleaning, and some minor plumbing repairs.

When it was finished, the house looked like a completely different property. Clean, bright, move-in ready.

## The First Tenant

I listed the property for rent at $1050 per month, splitting the difference between what I thought it could get and what I needed it to cash flow properly.

Within a week, I had three applications. I chose a young couple who both worked at the university—stable employment, good references, first month's rent and security deposit ready to go.

The day they moved in and handed me that first rent check was a moment I'll never forget. $1050. Not a huge amount of money, but it represented something much bigger than the dollar amount.

It was proof that the whole system worked. That I could find a property, analyze the numbers, secure funding, manage renovations, find tenants, and generate monthly income from a real estate investment.

## The Wholesale Opportunity

About three months after closing on the Broad Street property, Jennifer called me with a different kind of opportunity.

"Lee, I've got a situation that might interest you. I have a seller who needs to close in ten days—she's relocating for work. The house needs some work, but it's priced to move quickly. Are you interested in taking a look?"

The property was another small single-family house, this one needing more extensive repairs than I was ready to take on. But as I walked through it with Jennifer, calculating repair costs and potential after-repair value, I realized something: this could be a good deal for the right buyer, even if it wasn't right for me.

"Jennifer, what if I could find someone to buy this property from you? Someone who's looking for a fix-and-flip project?"

"You mean like a referral?"

"Sort of. More like I'd put it under contract and then find someone to buy the contract from me."

I was describing wholesaling without knowing that's what it was called. I'd heard M mention the concept, but I'd never seen it done.

"That's called wholesaling," Jennifer said. "It's perfectly legal as long as you're transparent about what you're doing. Are you licensed?"

"No, but I'm working on it."

"Well, in Georgia, you can assign contracts without a license as long as you're buying for your own account initially. If you want to make this work, you'd need to put the house under contract, then find someone to assign that contract to before closing."

## The $11,000 Education

I put the house under contract for $105,000, knowing it was worth probably $140,000 after repairs. My plan was to find an investor who wanted a fix-and-flip project and assign my contract to them for $116,000—giving me an $11,000 assignment fee.

Jennifer said she might know someone. "I've got a guy who buys everything in this area for fix-and-flip projects. He's always looking for deals."

When she called him, he was interested immediately. "I'll pay $116,000," he said. "When can we close?"

I couldn't believe it was that simple.

The closing was scheduled for the following Friday. The buyer would pay $116,000 to the seller, I would assign my contract for an $11,000 fee, and everyone would be happy.

## The Hand-Shaking Moment

The day of the closing, I was nervous in a completely different way than I'd been for my first purchase. This time, I wasn't putting my own money at risk—I was about to get paid for finding and contracting a good deal.

When the attorney handed me a check for $11,000, my hands were literally shaking.

This wasn't drug money. This wasn't stolen money. This was legitimate business income I'd earned by identifying an opportunity, putting it under contract, and connecting it with the right buyer.

I had made $11,000 in less than three weeks, using nothing but knowledge, hustle, and the ability to recognize a good deal.

Sitting in my car after the closing, holding that check, I had a realization that changed everything: if I could make $11,000 on one deal in three weeks, what could I make in a year? What could I make with better systems, more knowledge, stronger relationships?

## The Lightbulb Moment

That first wholesale deal taught me something crucial about real estate investing: **there are multiple ways to make money from the same market knowledge.**

I could buy properties to hold as rentals (like the Broad Street house). I could find properties for other investors and earn assignment fees (like the wholesale deal). I could potentially buy, fix, and flip properties myself.

Each strategy used the same core skills—finding properties, analyzing deals, understanding market values—but generated income in different ways and required different amounts of capital.

More importantly, I realized that real estate wasn't just about having money to invest. It was about having knowledge, systems, and relationships that allowed you to identify and capitalize on opportunities.

## House Money Hack: Start with Action, Not Perfection

The biggest lesson from my first deals was that you learn more from doing one deal than from analyzing a hundred deals.

I spent months studying real estate, reading books, analyzing properties online, and talking to Marcus about strategies. All of that education was valuable, but it wasn't until I actually put a property under contract that I really understood how the process worked.

**Here's the truth about getting started in real estate (or any business):**

**1. You'll never feel 100% ready.** There will always be more to learn, more money you wish you had, more experience you think you need. Waiting for perfect readiness is really just fear in disguise.

**2. The market will teach you faster than books.** Real deals with real deadlines and real money at stake teach you things that no amount of theoretical study can provide.

**3. Your first deal doesn't have to be your biggest deal.** Start small, learn the process, make your mistakes on a manageable scale, then use that experience to do bigger and better deals.

**4. Knowledge without action is just entertainment.** I knew dozens of people who could analyze real estate deals all day long but had never actually bought a property. Don't be an analyst—be an investor.

**5. The confidence comes from doing, not from knowing.** After my first successful purchase and my first wholesale deal, I felt like I could handle whatever came next. That confidence came from proven experience, not theoretical knowledge.

**The key is to start with deals that match your current skill level and financial capacity, then scale up as your experience grows.**

I didn't try to buy a 20-unit apartment building on my first deal. I bought a simple single-family house that I could understand, afford, and manage. That experience gave me the confidence and knowledge to tackle more complex opportunities.

**Action creates clarity. Clarity creates confidence. Confidence creates bigger action.**

**What's the smallest real estate deal you could do right now to get started?**

# PART III: THE SYSTEM

# CHAPTER 7

## Plastic Power Moves

That $11,000 check from my first wholesale deal was a revelation, but it also created a new problem: I was hooked. Not just on the money—though making more in three weeks than I used to make in three months was definitely motivating—but on the process. The hunt for deals, the analysis, the negotiation, the problem-solving. Real estate investing was like a game where you got paid to play.

But I was still running into the same fundamental limitation that had frustrated me before: capital. Each deal required money I didn't have, and while business credit had helped with my first purchase, I needed a more systematic way to fund multiple deals without depleting my cash reserves.

That's when David introduced me to a concept that would completely transform how I approached business financing: credit card stacking.

### The 0% Money Revolution

"Lee," David said during one of our monthly check-ins, "you did great on that first deal, but you're still thinking too small. You used one credit card for $10,000. What if I told you that you could access $50,000, $100,000, or more in 0% financing?"

"I'd say that sounds impossible."

"It's not only possible, it's systematic. The credit card companies are basically offering free money for 12-18 months to qualified businesses. The key is knowing how to access it strategically."

David explained that many business credit cards offered 0% introductory APR for 12-18 months on purchases or balance transfers. If you could get approved for multiple cards and use them strategically, you could essentially borrow large amounts of money interest-free for over a year.

"The beauty of this system," he said, "is that you're not getting traditional loans that require tax returns, bank statements, and extensive underwriting. You're getting approved based on your business credit profile and your ability to make payments."

## The Application Strategy

David taught me a systematic approach to applying for business credit cards that maximized approvals while minimizing negative impacts on my credit:

**Rule #1: Space applications properly.** Never apply for more than one card per month. Multiple applications in a short time period look desperate and hurt your credit score.

**Rule #2: Target the right lenders.** Different banks had different appetites for business lending. Chase, American Express, and Capital One were generally more aggressive than smaller banks.

**Rule #3: Have a plan for each card.** Don't apply for credit just to have it. Have specific business uses planned for each card before you apply.

**Rule #4: Manage utilization carefully.** Even with high limits, keeping balances below 30% of available credit was crucial for maintaining good credit scores.

**Rule #5: Pay strategically.** With 0% APR, you didn't need to pay balances off immediately, but you needed to have a clear plan for paying them off before the promotional period ended.

## The Six-Month Blitz

Over six months, I systematically applied for and was approved for six different business credit cards:

- Chase Ink Business Cash: $15,000 limit, 0% APR for 12 months
- American Express Business Gold: $25,000 limit, 0% APR for 15 months
- Capital One Spark Cash: $20,000 limit, 0% APR for 12 months
- Wells Fargo Business Platinum: $12,000 limit, 0% APR for 18 months
- Bank of America Business Cash: $18,000 limit, 0% APR for 12 months
- Discover Business: $10,000 limit, 0% APR for 14 months

Total available credit: $100,000 Average promotional period: 13.5 months Cost of capital: $0 (if managed properly)

## The Real Estate Acceleration

With access to $100,000 in 0% financing, everything changed. Instead of being able to afford one property every couple of years, I could potentially fund 4-5 deals simultaneously.

But David warned me about the importance of having solid systems in place: "This is powerful, but it's also dangerous if you don't manage it properly. You need to have clear plans for how each dollar will be used and how it will be repaid."

I developed a systematic approach:

### Property Acquisition Strategy:

- Use 20-25% credit card funding for down payments
- Focus on properties that would cash flow positive immediately
- Target properties that could be rented quickly with minimal renovation

### Renovation Funding:

- Use credit cards for all contractor payments and materials
- Track expenses carefully for business tax deductions
- Complete renovations quickly to get properties rent-ready

### Repayment Plan:

- Set aside first six months of rental income for credit card payments
- Use any wholesale or flip profits to pay down balances
- Refinance properties when possible to pay off credit cards

**The Travel Hack Discovery**

About three months into using this system, I made a discovery that would change how I thought about credit cards forever: I was earning massive amounts of rewards points.

Every dollar I spent on real estate—down payments, contractor fees, material purchases, property management expenses—was earning me 1-3 points per dollar spent. And since I was spending $50,000-$75,000 per month on real estate activities, I was accumulating points faster than I ever imagined possible.

Marcus was the first to point this out. "Dude, do you realize how many points you're earning on all this real estate spending?"

I hadn't really been paying attention to the rewards aspect—I was focused on the 0% financing. But when I logged into my credit card accounts and looked at my point balances, I was shocked.

In three months, I had earned:

- 75,000 Chase Ultimate Rewards points
- 50,000 American Express Membership Rewards points
- 45,000 Capital One Miles
- Plus thousands of points across other cards

"What do I do with all these points?" I asked Marcus.

"Man, you can travel anywhere in the world for free. First class flights, luxury hotels, the whole nine yards."

## The First-Class Education

That weekend, I spent hours researching travel rewards programs. What I discovered was that credit card points weren't just for domestic flights and budget hotels—they could be transferred to airline and hotel partners for premium travel experiences.

I learned about:

- **Transfer partners** that offered 1:1 point transfers to major airlines
- **Sweet spot redemptions** where points were worth 2-5 cents each instead of 1 cent
- **Business class and first class availability** using points
- **Luxury hotel stays** at a fraction of cash prices

My first redemption was a round-trip business class flight to London using 60,000 Chase Ultimate Rewards points. The cash price for that same ticket was $4,500. I had essentially gotten $4,500 worth of travel for free, using points I earned from business expenses I was going to have anyway.

That trip opened my eyes to a completely different lifestyle. Not just the luxury of business class travel, but the freedom that comes from being able to travel anywhere in the world without worrying about the cost.

## The System Integration

What made this strategy so powerful was how all the pieces worked together:

Real Estate Deals → Credit Card Spending → Points Accumulation → Free Travel

Every property I bought generated points. Every renovation I funded generated points. Every business expense generated points. And those points translated to travel experiences that would have cost tens of thousands of dollars in cash.

But more importantly, the credit cards were enabling me to scale my real estate business much faster than would have been possible with cash alone.

In my first year using this system, I:

- Purchased 4 rental properties
- Completed 3 wholesale deals
- Earned over 300,000 rewards points
- Traveled to 6 countries in business or first class
- Generated over $4,000 per month in rental income

**The Dubai Discovery**

The ultimate test of this system came when I decided to explore international real estate investing. I had heard about opportunities in Dubai through some real estate forums, but I hadn't seriously considered it because international deals seemed too complex and expensive to pursue.

But with my point balances, I could fly to Dubai in first class for basically free. The business class ticket I booked would have cost $8,000 in cash, but I used 80,000 American Express points.

During that trip, I discovered that Dubai's real estate market operated very differently from the U.S. market. Many properties were sold pre-construction with payment plans that allowed you to pay in installments over 2-3 years. And crucially, many developers accepted credit card payments.

I ended up putting a deposit on a luxury apartment in Dubai Marina using Chase. The total purchase price was $250,000, but I was able to use credit cards for a significant portion of the down payment and installment payments.

What blew my mind was that I was earning points on an international real estate purchase. I was literally getting free flights to visit my international property using points I earned from buying the property.

**The Compound Effect**

By year two of using this system, the compound effects were becoming obvious:

More Properties → More Rental Income → More Cash Flow → Ability to Handle Larger Credit Balances

More Credit Card Usage → More Points → More Travel → More International Opportunities

More Experience → Better Deal Recognition → Higher Profits → Faster Growth

The system was feeding itself. Each successful deal made the next deal easier. Each trip opened up new opportunities. Each point earned was essentially free money for experiences I'd never have been able to afford with cash.

**House Money Hack: Turn Expenses Into Assets**

The credit card stacking strategy taught me one of the most important lessons about building wealth: **every expense is an opportunity if you structure it correctly.**

Most people think about credit cards as either good or bad. Dave Ramsey disciples see them as dangerous debt traps. Points chasers see them as ways to get free flights. But I learned to see them as **business tools** that could serve multiple purposes simultaneously.

**Here's how to implement this strategy safely:**

**1. Start with a solid foundation.** Don't attempt credit card stacking until you have good personal credit (700+), established business credit, and proven cash flow from your investments.

**2. Apply systematically.** Space applications 30-45 days apart. Target cards with the longest 0% promotional periods and the best rewards programs.

**3. Use for planned expenses only.** Never use credit cards for consumption or lifestyle inflation. Only use them for business expenses you were going to have anyway.

**4. Track everything meticulously.** Know exactly when each promotional period ends, what your minimum payments are, and how much you need to pay to avoid interest.

**5. Have multiple exit strategies.** Don't rely on just one source of repayment. Have rental income, business profits, and potential refinancing all as backup plans.

**6. Optimize for both financing and rewards.** Choose cards that offer 0% financing AND strong rewards programs. You can fund your business and earn travel at the same time.

**The key insight is that business credit cards can serve as both capital and currency—capital for your investments and currency for your lifestyle.**

When managed properly, this strategy allows you to:

- Scale your business faster than cash flow alone would allow
- Travel the world at a fraction of the normal cost
- Build credit history and increase future borrowing capacity
- Generate tax-deductible business expenses
- Create multiple streams of value from the same spending

**The danger is obvious: if you can't manage the payments or don't have reliable income to service the debt, you can destroy your credit and your business.**

But when used as part of a systematic wealth-building strategy, credit cards become one of the most powerful tools available to entrepreneurs and real estate investors.

**Your business expenses are happening anyway. Why not turn them into first-class flights and faster business growth?**

# CHAPTER 8

## Out the Mud, Into the Market

By early 2019, I had built something I'd never imagined possible three years earlier: a systematic wealth-building machine. Four rental properties generating $3,800 per month in cash flow. A business credit profile that gave me access to over $150,000 in financing. A travel rewards system that had taken me to twelve countries in business class. And most importantly, the confidence that comes from proving a system works.

But I was starting to feel constrained by the Athens market. Don't get me wrong—Athens had been perfect for learning the business and building my foundation. But I was ready for bigger opportunities, and I was starting to think beyond just single-family rentals.

That's when three conversations changed the trajectory of my entire real estate career.

## Conversation #1: The Property Manager Revolution

The first conversation was with Sarah Martinez, a property management company owner I'd been working with for about six months. I'd hired her company to manage two of my rental properties after realizing that collecting rent, handling maintenance calls, and dealing with tenant issues was eating up more time than I wanted to spend.

"Lee," she said during one of our quarterly reviews, "I need to tell you something. You're doing this wrong."

That wasn't what I expected to hear from someone I was paying to help me.

"What do you mean?"

"You're too involved in the day-to-day operations. You're calling me about maintenance requests, asking about tenant showings, wanting updates on rent collection. That's my job. You hired me so you wouldn't have to do those things."

She was right. Even though I was paying for property management, I was still acting like I needed to manage the managers.

"Here's what successful real estate investors do," Sarah continued. "They set up systems, hire good people, and then focus on finding the next deal. They treat real estate like a business, not a hobby."

"The most successful client I have owns 47 units. You know how often he calls me? Maybe once a quarter, just to review the numbers. He spends his time finding new properties and raising capital, not worrying about whether someone's toilet got fixed."

That conversation was a wake-up call. I was thinking too small and staying too involved in operations that other people could handle better than me.

## The System Overhaul

Based on Sarah's advice, I completely restructured how I approached property management:

**Digital Rent Collection:** All tenants were required to pay rent through an online portal. No more checks, no more cash, no more wondering if rent had been paid.

**Maintenance Automation:** Tenants submitted maintenance requests through the online system. Sarah's team handled everything under $500 automatically, only calling me for major repairs.

**Automated Listings:** When properties became vacant, they were automatically listed on Zillow, Apartments.com, and other platforms with professional photos and virtual tours.

**Financial Reporting:** I received detailed monthly reports showing income, expenses, occupancy rates, and maintenance issues across all properties.

This system freed up about 10-15 hours per week that I had been spending on property management tasks. Time I could now spend finding new deals, building relationships, and scaling the business.

## Conversation #2: The Mentor's Challenge

The second conversation was with David, my credit mentor, during one of our monthly check-ins.

"Lee, I've been watching what you're building, and I'm impressed. But I think you're playing it too safe."

"What do you mean?"

"You've got access to $150,000 in credit, but you're using it to buy $100,000 houses one at a time. You could be using that same credit to buy a $500,000 apartment building, or commercial property, or out-of-state deals with better cash flow."

David pulled out a calculator and started running numbers.

"Let's say you keep doing what you're doing. You buy one $100,000 property per year. In ten years, you'll own ten properties worth maybe $1.5 million total. That's good, but it's not life-changing wealth."

"Now let's say you use that same credit capacity to buy bigger deals. Maybe a $400,000 duplex that generates twice the cash flow. Or a small apartment building. Or properties in markets with better appreciation potential. In ten years, you could own $5-10 million in real estate."

He was challenging me to think bigger, take more calculated risks, and use my growing resources more aggressively.

### Conversation #3: The International Awakening

The third conversation happened on a plane to London. I was using points for another business class trip, sitting next to a woman named Priya Patel who was reading real estate investment magazines.

"Are you in real estate?" I asked during our layover.

"Yes, but probably not the kind you're thinking of. I buy property in Dubai and other international markets for American investors."

"How does that work?"

What Priya explained over the next two hours changed how I thought about real estate investing entirely.

"Dubai is building the future," she said. "They're creating a global financial hub from scratch, and real estate is one of the primary vehicles for attracting international investment."

She showed me photos on her phone of construction projects that looked like something from a science fiction movie. Artificial islands, underwater hotels, buildings that twisted as they rose into the sky.

"The best part is how the financing works. Many developers accept payment plans that let you buy pre-construction properties with minimal money down, then pay in installments over 2-3 years. And they accept credit cards for payments."

Credit cards? For international real estate? I was intrigued.

"I have clients who have used credit card funding to build international real estate portfolios worth millions of dollars. The key is understanding the markets, the legal structures, and the payment systems."

By the time we landed in London, I had her business card and a completely new perspective on what was possible with real estate investing.

## The Dubai Deep Dive

Six months later, I was on a plane to Dubai. Not just for vacation—this was a business scouting trip to understand the international real estate market that Priya had introduced me to.

Dubai in 2020 was unlike anywhere I'd ever been. Construction cranes covered the skyline. New projects were being announced weekly. International investors from every continent were buying properties sight unseen.

What I discovered was that Dubai's real estate market was designed specifically to attract international investment:

**Developer Financing:** Most properties were sold pre-construction with payment plans that required 10-20% down, then installments over 2-3 years.

**Credit Card Acceptance:** Many developers accepted credit card payments, which meant I could use my business credit to fund international deals.

**No Income Verification:** Unlike U.S. real estate, Dubai developers were primarily concerned with your ability to make the scheduled payments, not your traditional income documentation.

**Residency Benefits:** Property ownership above certain thresholds qualified you for Dubai residency, which opened up additional business and banking opportunities.

## The First International Deal

After three days of looking at projects, I found one that met my criteria: a luxury apartment in Dubai Marina, scheduled for completion in Q1 2008.

Purchase price: $250,000 Down payment: $25,000 (10%) Installment payments: $1,000 every month until I reached half: $125,000. The rest would be due upon completion of the project in which by then I could get a loan or just pay off completely.

What made this deal attractive wasn't just the property itself—it was the payment structure. I could use credit cards for the down payment and installment payments, essentially using 0% financing to fund an international real estate investment.

More importantly, Dubai properties were appreciating rapidly. Comparable completed units in the same building were already selling for $300,000+, suggesting immediate equity gain upon completion.

I used three different business credit cards for the $25,000 down payment, earning 95,000 points in the process—enough for multiple international business class flights.

## The Systematic Expansion

The Dubai purchase taught me something crucial about scaling real estate investing: **geographic diversification could amplify returns while reducing risk.**

Instead of being limited to Athens, Georgia real estate prices and rental yields, I could now access:

**Higher Appreciation Markets:** Dubai properties were appreciating 20-30% annually vs. 3-5% in Athens

**Better Cash Flow Markets:** Some international markets offered rental yields of 8-12% vs. 5-7% in my local market

**Currency Diversification:** International properties provided hedge against U.S. dollar fluctuations

**Tax Advantages:** International real estate offered different depreciation and tax structures

**Lifestyle Benefits:** Owning property in Dubai meant I had a reason to travel there regularly, expanding my global network and investment knowledge

## The Credit Card Scaling Strategy

The Dubai deal proved that credit cards could be used for much larger real estate transactions than I'd previously imagined. Over the next 18 months, I systematically expanded this approach:

**Deal #1:** $450,000 duplex in Atlanta using $90,000 in credit cards for down payment **Deal #2:** $325,000 apartment building in Birmingham using $65,000 in credit cards **Deal #3:** Second Dubai property ($750,000) using credit cards for all installment payments **Deal #4:** Commercial property in Athens using credit cards for renovation funding

Each deal generated significant rewards points, which I used for business travel to scout new markets, attend real estate conferences, and visit my international properties.

**The Cash Flow Explosion**

By late 2007, my real estate portfolio was generating over $12,000 per month in positive cash flow:

- Athens properties: $3,800/month
- Atlanta duplex: $2,200/month
- Birmingham apartments: $3,500/month
- Dubai projected rental (upon completion): $2,800/month

This cash flow was enough to cover all my credit card payments, personal living expenses, and still leave money for reinvestment.

More importantly, the equity gains from appreciation had increased my net worth by over $400,000 in two years.

**The Land Back Home**

With my cash flow stabilized and my credit capacity proven, I decided to make an investment that was more emotional than financial: buying land back in Longview, Texas.

Not for immediate development or cash flow, but as a long-term hold and a connection to my roots. I found 20 acres outside town that reminded me of the land my grandparents had farmed, priced at $85,000.

I used a combination of cash flow from my rental properties and a small business credit line to purchase it outright. No plans for immediate development—just ownership of a piece of East Texas that I could eventually pass down or develop when the timing was right.

**House Money Hack: Scale Through Systems, Not Just Size**

The transition from small local deals to larger national and international deals taught me that scaling isn't just about buying bigger properties— it's about building better systems.

**Here's the framework I developed for systematic scaling:**

**1. Perfect Your Local Market First** Master your home market before expanding geographically. Understand the numbers, build relationships, and prove your systems work at a smaller scale.

**2. Systematize Operations Before Scaling** Don't try to manage more properties until you've systematized the management of your current properties. Automation and delegation are prerequisites for scaling.

**3. Use Technology as a Force Multiplier** Digital rent collection, online maintenance requests, automated listing systems, and electronic document management allow you to handle many more properties without proportionally increasing your time investment.

**4. Expand Credit Capacity Systematically** As your business grows and your cash flow increases, systematically apply for additional business credit lines. Use success to build more capacity for future success.

**5. Diversify Geographically for Better Returns** Don't limit yourself to your local market if better opportunities exist elsewhere. Use technology and professional networks to invest in markets with superior cash flow or appreciation potential.

**6. Think Globally, Execute Systematically** International real estate can offer superior returns and diversification, but only if you understand the legal, financial, and operational differences in each market.

**The key insight is that scaling requires increasing your capacity across multiple dimensions simultaneously: financial capacity, operational capacity, knowledge capacity, and relationship capacity.**

You can't just increase one element—you need to grow them all in parallel to scale sustainably.

**Geographic arbitrage became one of my most powerful wealth-building tools—using credit and systems developed in one market to access better opportunities in other markets.**

This approach allowed me to benefit from:

- Athens cash flow to fund Dubai appreciation
- Dubai credit card points to fund U.S. market research trips
- U.S. business credit to access international opportunities
- International experience to identify better U.S. deals

**Your local market is your training ground. The global market is your playing field. Are you ready to expand beyond your zip code?**

# CHAPTER 9

# The Coach on the Corner

By 2023, I owned properties in two countries, had a portfolio generating over $15,000 per month in cash flow, and could travel anywhere in the world in first class using points. By most measures, I had achieved the financial freedom I'd dreamed about when I first got on that Greyhound bus in Texas.

But something was missing.

I was making money, but I wasn't making meaning. I was building wealth, but I wasn't building legacy. I had achieved independence, but I hadn't found purpose.

That changed when I got a phone call from Coach Ward at Clarke Central High School in Athens.

**The Unexpected Invitation**

"Lee, this is Coach Ward. I got your number from Alex. He said you might be interested in helping with our track and cross country program."

I knew Coach Ward by reputation—he'd been coaching in Athens for over twenty years and had developed several athletes who went on to compete at the collegiate level. But I had no idea why he was calling me.

"alex mentioned that you ran at UGA and that you're doing well in business. We're looking for someone to help coach our distance runners, and he thought you might be a good fit."

Coaching? I hadn't thought about coaching since my competitive days ended. But as Coach Ward described the program, something stirred in me that I hadn't felt in years.

"These kids have talent," he said, "but most of them don't have examples of what's possible. They need to see someone who came from a similar background and made something of himself."

## The Full-Circle Moment

Clarke Central High School was less than a mile from the University of Georgia campus where I'd run track as a student. It was in the same community where I now owned rental properties. Many of the kids I'd be coaching lived in the same neighborhoods where my tenants lived.

But what really struck me was the similarity between these kids and my younger self. Most of them came from working-class families. Many had parents who worked multiple jobs to make ends meet. Some lived in single-parent households or with grandparents.

They had talent, but they didn't have exposure. They had dreams, but they didn't have examples of how those dreams could become reality.

When I walked onto the track for my first practice, I saw myself fifteen years earlier—hungry, determined, but not really understanding what was possible beyond the immediate goal of maybe earning a college scholarship.

## The First Practice

"Coach Patterson," Coach Ward announced to the team, "ran at UGA and is going to be working with our distance runners."

Fifteen kids, ages 14-18, mostly Black and Hispanic, looking at me with a mixture of curiosity and skepticism. I was wearing a polo shirt and nice pants—clearly not dressed for practice—and probably looked more like a parent than a coach.

"How fast did you run in college?" one of the kids asked.

I gave them my times, which were respectable but not legendary. I could see them doing mental calculations, trying to figure out if I was fast enough to teach them anything.

"Times don't matter as much as you think," I told them. "What matters is understanding that running is just the beginning. The discipline you learn from training, the goal-setting skills you develop, the mental toughness you build—that stuff will serve you for the rest of your life."

They looked at me like I was speaking a foreign language.

## The Real Education Begins

Over the first few weeks of practice, I learned as much about some these kids as they learned about running. Their stories were familiar—single mothers working two jobs, fathers who weren't around, financial stress that made every decision complicated.

But I also saw something that reminded me of myself at their age: an understanding that sports could be a way out, even if they didn't fully understand what "out" looked like.

"Coach P," one of the kids asked after practice one day, "what do you do when you're not coaching?"

"I'm in real estate," I said.

"Like, you sell houses?"

"Sort of. I buy houses and rent them out to people. I also invest in properties in other countries."

The conversation that followed opened my eyes to how little these kids knew about building wealth, creating passive income, or thinking beyond traditional employment.

They understood working hard—most of them had jobs after school or helped take care of younger siblings. But they'd never been exposed to concepts like assets vs. liabilities, compound interest, or building equity.

**The Teachable Moments**

I started incorporating life lessons into our training sessions. During long runs, when we had 30-45 minutes of steady pace running, I'd share stories about business, investing, and building wealth.

"See that house over there?" I'd say as we ran past one of my rental properties. "I own that. The family living there pays me rent every month, which helps pay for this house and that house and the one over there too."

"How much money do you make from that?" they'd ask.

"That house brings in about $900 a month. After expenses, I probably clear $300. But here's the beautiful thing—I don't have to show up every day to earn that $300. The house makes money whether I'm sleeping, traveling, or coaching you all."

I could see their minds working, trying to understand how this was possible.

## The Asset vs. Liability Lesson

One day, as we were stretching after practice, I noticed several of the kids talking about new shoes, new phones, and cars they wanted to buy when they turned sixteen.

"Let me ask you all a question," I said. "What's the difference between an asset and a liability?"

Blank stares.

"An asset puts money in your pocket. A liability takes money out of your pocket. Those new Jordans you want? That's a liability. That car you're saving up for? Probably a liability. That house I showed you? That's an asset."

I started using their own experiences to illustrate the concepts.

"Marcus, you work at McDonald's after school, right? How much do you make an hour?"

"$7.25."

"So if you want those $200 shoes, how many hours do you have to work to afford them?"

"About 28 hours, after taxes."

"And how much value do those shoes have after you wear them for six months?"

"Maybe $50?"

"So you're trading 28 hours of your life for something that loses 75% of its value. What if instead of buying those shoes, you saved that $200 and learned how to invest it?"

## The Investment Club

These conversations led to the formation of an informal "investment club" among the team. After practice twice a week, any kids who were interested could stay for an extra 30 minutes while I taught them basic financial literacy concepts.

We covered:

- The difference between assets and liabilities
- How compound interest works
- Why starting early with investing gives you huge advantages
- How credit works and why it matters

- Basic real estate investing concepts
- The importance of multiple income streams

I kept the lessons simple and practical, using examples from their own lives and the community around them.

**The Resistance and the Breakthrough**

Not all the kids were interested initially. Some thought it was boring. Others couldn't see how any of this applied to their current situations.

"Coach P," one of them said, "this stuff sounds cool, but I need to worry about getting a scholarship first. I can't think about buying houses when my family might get evicted from ours."

That comment stopped me in my tracks. I realized I was talking to kids who were dealing with immediate survival issues about long-term wealth building. I needed to meet them where they were.

"You're absolutely right," I said. "Getting a scholarship should be your first priority. But here's the thing—the same discipline and goal-setting skills that will get you a scholarship are the same skills you'll need to build wealth later. And the sooner you understand how money works, the better decisions you'll make when you do have money."

That's when I started connecting athletics to wealth building in more direct ways:

- "Training consistently for months to see results = investing consistently for years to build wealth"
- "Setting PR goals and tracking progress = setting financial goals and tracking net worth"

- "Dealing with setbacks and injuries = handling business challenges and market downturns"
- "Working as a team = building business partnerships and networks"

## The Success Stories

Over three years of coaching, I watched several kids have breakthrough moments that went beyond athletics:

**Jasmine** started a small business doing hair for her classmates and saved enough money to buy her first car with cash instead of taking out a loan.

**Beck** got a full scholarship to Georgia Southern and used his understanding of assets vs. liabilities to avoid the credit card debt that trapped many of his college friends.

**Dominic** started investing $25 per month in a Roth IRA at age 16, understanding that starting early would give him decades of compound growth.

**Kaitlyn** chose her college major partly based on earning potential and career stability, not just personal interest, because she understood the importance of building income-generating skills.

These weren't dramatic transformations, but they were mindset shifts that would compound over decades.

## The Community Impact

What surprised me was how my involvement with the track team started affecting my relationship with the broader community. Parents started recognizing me as "Coach P" instead of just "the landlord."

Kids I coached would wave when they saw me around town. Teachers at the school started asking me to speak to their classes about entrepreneurship and financial literacy.

I realized I was becoming woven into the fabric of the community in a way that just owning property never could have achieved.

## The Personal Transformation

But the biggest change was in me. Coaching gave me something that all my real estate success hadn't provided: a sense of purpose that went beyond personal gain.

Don't get me wrong—I loved building wealth, traveling the world, and achieving financial freedom. But teaching kids about possibilities they'd never considered, watching them develop confidence and discipline, seeing them make better decisions because of conversations we'd had during practice—that was fulfilling in a completely different way.

I started looking forward to practice as much as I looked forward to closing real estate deals. The kids' improvements in running times excited me as much as my portfolio's cash flow improvements.

## The Integration

By 2020, coaching had become fully integrated into my identity and my business model. The time I spent at the track wasn't separate from my wealth-building activities—it was part of them.

Coaching kept me connected to the community where I invested. It gave me perspective on long-term thinking and patience. It reminded me that success wasn't just about accumulating assets, but about creating value for other people.

Most importantly, it gave me a laboratory for testing and refining the principles I'd learned about discipline, goal-setting, and systematic improvement.

### House Money Hack: Find Your Purpose Beyond Profit

Coaching taught me that sustainable wealth building requires more than just financial strategies—it requires a sense of purpose that connects your success to something bigger than yourself.

### Here's why this matters for wealth building:

1. **Purpose Provides Persistence** When real estate deals fall through, markets decline, or business challenges arise, having a deeper purpose helps you push through difficulties that might otherwise make you quit.

2. **Community Connection Creates Opportunities** Being known for contribution, not just accumulation, opens doors and creates relationships that purely transactional approaches can't access.

3. **Teaching Strengthens Understanding** Explaining financial concepts to teenagers forced me to understand them more clearly myself, which made me a better investor and businessperson.

4. **Long-term Perspective Improves Decision Making** Coaching kids who won't see the full benefits of their training for years taught me patience and long-term thinking that improved my investment decisions.

**5. Values Alignment Increases Satisfaction** Wealth without purpose can feel empty. Having a mission that goes beyond personal gain makes financial success more meaningful and sustainable.

**The key is finding a way to serve others that also aligns with and enhances your wealth-building activities.**

For me, coaching connected perfectly with real estate investing:

- Both required long-term thinking and patience
- Both involved teaching and mentoring relationships
- Both were rooted in the same community
- Both required discipline and systematic improvement
- Both created positive impacts that extended beyond immediate financial returns

**Your wealth-building journey needs an anchor that goes deeper than money. What community could you serve while building your empire?**

The kids I coached taught me that true wealth isn't just about what you accumulate—it's about what you contribute. And contribution, it turns out, is one of the best investments you can make.

# CHAPTER 10

# Build It Without Burnout

By 2023, I had everything I thought I wanted when I first started investing in real estate. Twenty-three properties across four markets generating over $18,000 per month in cash flow. International investments in Dubai that had appreciated significantly. A coaching position that gave me purpose and community connection. And enough travel points to fly anywhere in the world in first class.

But I was also exhausted.

Managing properties across multiple states and countries, even with good property management companies, required constant attention. Coordinating maintenance issues, approving major repairs, reviewing financial reports, and dealing with problem tenants was consuming more time than I wanted to spend on operational details.

I was successful, but I wasn't free. I had built a business that owned me instead of a business that I owned.

That's when I learned the most important lesson of my entire real estate career: **systems create freedom, but only if you actually use them.**

## The Wake-Up Call

The wake-up call came during what should have been a relaxing vacation in Greece. I was sitting on a beautiful beach in Santorini, supposedly enjoying a week off, but I was on my phone dealing with a plumbing emergency at my Atlanta duplex.

The property manager was calling me about a $3,000 repair that needed approval. The tenant was texting me directly about the inconvenience. My contractor in Athens was asking about scheduling for a different property. And my Dubai property manager was emailing about rental market changes that might affect my international investment.

Here I was, in one of the most beautiful places on earth, using points I'd earned from my real estate business, but unable to enjoy it because the business was demanding my constant attention.

That night, sitting on my hotel balcony overlooking the Aegean Sea, I made a decision: I was going to systematize every aspect of my real estate business so that it could run without my daily involvement.

## The Digital Revolution

When I got back from Greece, I spent two weeks researching property management software, digital communication tools, and automation systems that could reduce my operational involvement.

What I discovered was that the real estate industry had been transformed by technology while I'd been focused on acquiring properties. Tools existed that could automate most of the tasks I was handling manually.

**Digital Rent Collection** I implemented a system where all tenants had to pay rent through an online portal. No more checks, no more cash, no more wondering if payments had been made. Rent was automatically deposited into my business accounts, late fees were automatically applied, and I received automated reports on collection rates.

**Maintenance Request Systems** Instead of tenants calling me or property managers about maintenance issues, they submitted requests through an online system that automatically routed them to appropriate contractors, tracked completion times, and maintained records of all work performed.

**Automated Listings and Applications** When properties became vacant, they were automatically listed on multiple platforms with professional photos, virtual tours, and detailed descriptions. Prospective tenants could submit applications online, complete background checks digitally, and even sign leases electronically.

**Financial Dashboard Integration** All properties fed into a single dashboard that showed me income, expenses, occupancy rates, maintenance costs, and profitability across my entire portfolio in real-time.

### The Property Manager Evolution

But the biggest game-changer wasn't technology—it was evolving my relationship with property management companies from service providers to true business partners.

Instead of micromanaging every decision, I established clear protocols and approval limits:

**Tier 1 Decisions (Under $500):** Property managers could handle automatically without my approval **Tier 2 Decisions ($500-$2,000):** Property managers could approve with email notification
 **Tier 3 Decisions (Over $2,000):** Required my approval, but with detailed analysis and recommendations

This system meant that 90% of operational decisions were handled without my involvement, while I retained control over major financial decisions.

## The Communication Boundaries

I also established strict communication boundaries:

**Emergency Contact:** Only for situations requiring immediate action (fire, flood, injury) **Weekly Reports:** Standardized summary of all activities across all properties **Monthly Reviews:** Detailed financial analysis and strategic planning **Quarterly Meetings:** In-person or video call strategic planning sessions

No more random phone calls about minor issues. No more texts from tenants. No more emails about routine maintenance. Everything flowed through established channels with appropriate priority levels.

## The International Automation

Managing my Dubai property from the United States required even more sophisticated systems. I worked with a property management company that specialized in international investors and had robust digital infrastructure.

They provided:

- **Monthly video property inspections** sent via email
- **Digital rent collection** in multiple currencies
- **Automated lease renewals** with market rate adjustments
- **Detailed financial reporting** in U.S. dollar equivalents
- **24/7 emergency response** that didn't require my involvement

The result was that my international property required less of my time and attention than some of my domestic properties.

**The Content Creation Opportunity**

With my real estate business running systematically, I had something I hadn't experienced since my early property management days: time freedom. But instead of just enjoying the passive income, I started thinking about what to do with this newfound time.

That's when I discovered the digital space.

I'd been helping kids on my track team understand real estate and financial literacy for three years. I'd been successfully using credit and alternative financing for five years. I'd been building a diverse real estate portfolio for seven years.

Maybe other people could benefit from what I'd learned.

**The First YouTube Videos**

I started simple: uploading basic educational videos about real estate investing to YouTube. "How to Analyze a Rental Property," "Understanding Business Credit for Real Estate," "My First Real Estate Deal Breakdown."

The production quality was terrible—I was filming with my phone in my kitchen—but the content was solid because it was based on real experience, not theoretical knowledge.

To my surprise, people started watching. And commenting. And asking questions.

Within six months, I had 500 subscribers. Within a year, I had 2,000. The videos were generating ad revenue, but more importantly, they were generating leads from people who wanted to learn more about my strategies.

**The Course Creation**

The YouTube comments kept asking the same questions:

- "How exactly do you use business credit for real estate?"
- "Can you show the step-by-step process?"
- "Do you have a course that teaches this system?"

I didn't have a course, but I realized I had something better: a proven system that I'd used to build a multi-million dollar real estate portfolio.

So I created one. "Credit to Real Estate: The Complete System."

The course covered everything I'd learned about:

- Credit repair and optimization
- Business credit establishment
- Real estate analysis and acquisition
- Property management automation
- International investing basics
- Travel hacking for real estate investors

I priced it at $497 and launched it to my small email list of about 300 people.

I sold 47 copies in the first week.

## The Community Building

The course students started asking for ongoing support and community connection. They wanted to share deals they were analyzing, ask questions about specific situations, and connect with other people using similar strategies.

So I created a private Facebook group for course members. What started as customer support evolved into a thriving community of real estate investors sharing knowledge, resources, and opportunities.

The community grew to over 1,000 members within eighteen months. They were posting about their deals, sharing contractor recommendations, partnering on investments, and even meeting up for local real estate networking events.

## The Coaching Evolution

As the community grew, some members wanted more personalized guidance. They were willing to pay for one-on-one coaching or small group mentorship.

I started offering monthly group coaching calls for $97 per month. The calls were designed to answer specific questions, review deals, and provide ongoing accountability for course members.

The coaching program quickly grew to 150 paying members, generating an additional $14,000+ per month in recurring revenue.

## The Mastermind Development

The most successful students wanted even more intensive support. They were ready to invest $5,000-$10,000 for access to my inner circle, advanced strategies, and direct mentorship.

I created a high-level mastermind program limited to 25 people. The program included:

- Quarterly in-person meetups
- Monthly group video calls
- Direct access to me via private messaging
- Deal review and partnership opportunities
- International investment trip opportunities

The mastermind generated $125,000 in revenue in its first year and created a network of serious investors who started partnering on larger deals.

**The Speaking and Partnerships**

Success in the digital space led to speaking opportunities at real estate conferences, podcast interviews, and partnership opportunities with other educators and investors.

These activities generated additional revenue streams:

- Speaking fees: $5,000-$15,000 per event
- Affiliate partnerships: $2,000-$5,000 per month
- Joint venture opportunities: $10,000-$50,000 per project

But more importantly, they positioned me as an authority in the real estate education space and created opportunities for even larger business developments.

**The Five-Day Challenge**

By 20254, I had built a comprehensive digital business around real estate education. But I wanted to create something that could serve people who weren't ready for paid courses—a free, high-value training that would introduce people to my strategies while building trust and demonstrating expertise.

The "Credit to Real Estate 5-Day Challenge" was designed to teach my complete system over five days of free training:

**Day 1:** Credit Foundation and Business Setup **Day 2:** Finding and Analyzing Deals
 **Day 3:** Funding Strategies and Applications **Day 4:** Property Management and Automation **Day 5:** Scaling and Advanced Strategies

The challenge attracted over 2,000 participants in its first iteration and became the primary lead generation tool for all my other programs.

**House Money Hack: Build Systems That Buy Back Your Time**

The transition from hands-on real estate investor to automated business owner taught me that the ultimate luxury isn't money—it's time freedom.

**Here's the framework I developed for building wealth without burnout:**

**1. Automate Everything Possible** If a task can be systematized and automated, do it. Digital rent collection, maintenance request systems, and financial reporting should run without your daily involvement.

**2. Delegate What Can't Be Automated** Hire property managers, virtual assistants, contractors, and other service providers who can handle operational tasks better than you can.

**3. Create Clear Decision-Making Protocols** Establish approval limits and decision-making criteria so that most operational decisions can be made without your involvement.

**4. Build Multiple Income Streams** Don't rely only on rental income. Create digital products, coaching programs, and other revenue streams that can scale without proportional time investment.

**5. Leverage Your Experience** Your knowledge and systems have value beyond just your own portfolio. Teaching others what you've learned can become a significant revenue stream.

**6. Use Technology as a Force Multiplier** The right software and systems can allow you to manage a large portfolio with less time than you used to spend managing a small portfolio.

**The goal isn't just to build wealth—it's to build wealth that gives you the freedom to live the life you actually want.**

For me, that meant being able to:

- Travel internationally for weeks without worrying about my properties
- Coach high school kids without rushing to handle business calls
- Create digital content and build online communities
- Pursue new investment opportunities without being overwhelmed by existing operations
- Sleep well knowing that my businesses could run effectively without my constant attention

**True wealth isn't just about the size of your portfolio—it's about the freedom that portfolio provides.**

If your wealth-building activities are consuming all your time and energy, you're building a job, not building freedom.

**What systems could you implement today to buy back an hour of your time tomorrow?**

# PART IV:
# THE BLUEPRINT

# CHAPTER 11

## House Money Principles

A fter eight years of building my real estate empire—from that first $11,000 wholesale check to a portfolio generating over $25,000 per month in passive income across multiple countries—I've learned that success in real estate isn't about luck, connections, or even starting capital.

It's about understanding and applying a systematic approach that anyone can learn and implement.

Whether you're starting with perfect credit or damaged credit, whether you have $50,000 saved or $500 in your checking account, whether you're 22 or 52, the principles remain the same. The timeline might be different, the specific tactics might vary, but the underlying system works regardless of your starting point.

This chapter breaks down the complete "House Money" system—the exact framework I've used to build wealth, travel the world, and create the freedom to coach kids, build digital businesses, and pursue opportunities most people only dream about.

**Principle #1: Credit is Your Foundation, Not Your Limitation**

Most people think about credit backward. They see their current credit score as a limitation that determines what they can or cannot do. But credit is actually a skill that can be developed, optimized, and leveraged strategically.

**The Credit Foundation Framework:**

**Personal Credit Optimization (0-6 months):**

- Pull all three credit reports and create a master improvement plan
- Dispute any inaccurate information using proper documentation
- Negotiate pay-for-delete agreements with collection agencies
- Pay down existing balances to below 30% utilization (ideally below 10%)
- Set up automatic payments to ensure perfect payment history going forward
- Target credit score of 700+ before moving to business credit

**Business Credit Establishment (3-12 months):**

- Form a legitimate business entity (LLC or Corporation) with proper state registration
- Obtain an EIN (Employer Identification Number) from the IRS
- Open business banking with a regional or national bank
- Establish a professional business address (not your home address)
- Set up a dedicated business phone line with professional voicemail
- Build trade references with vendors that report to business credit bureaus

- Apply for business credit cards starting with smaller banks, then major issuers

**Credit Utilization Strategy:**

- Maintain personal credit utilization below 10% across all cards
- Use business credit for business expenses only—never for personal consumption
- Pay balances strategically to maximize credit score impact
- Apply for new credit cards every 60-90 days (never more frequently)
- Track credit limits, promotional periods, and payment due dates meticulously

**Advanced Credit Tactics:**

- Request credit limit increases every 6 months on existing cards
- Use balance transfer offers to extend 0% promotional periods
- Stack multiple 0% APR cards for large real estate transactions
- Maintain strong business credit separate from personal credit

**Principle #2: Real Estate Analysis is Math, Not Emotion**

The difference between successful real estate investors and people who lose money in real estate is that successful investors buy assets, while unsuccessful investors buy properties that make them feel good.

**The 1% Rule Framework:**

The monthly rental income should equal at least 1% of the total purchase price (including purchase price plus major repairs needed).

Example: $100,000 purchase price → Minimum $1,000 monthly rent required

This rule ensures positive cash flow in most markets and provides a buffer for unexpected expenses, vacancies, and market fluctuations.

**Complete Deal Analysis Process:**

**Step 1: Property Evaluation**

- Location desirability and rental demand
- Property condition and major repair needs
- Comparable sales (what similar properties have sold for)
- Comparable rents (what similar properties rent for)
- Property taxes, insurance costs, and HOA fees

**Step 2: Financial Analysis**

- Total acquisition cost (purchase + repairs + closing costs)
- Monthly income potential (conservative rental estimate)
- Monthly expenses (mortgage, taxes, insurance, management, maintenance, vacancy allowance)
- Cash flow projection (income minus all expenses)
- Return on investment calculation (annual cash flow divided by total invested)

**Step 3: Exit Strategy Planning**

- Hold for rental income (cash flow strategy)
- Sell after improvements (fix and flip strategy)

- Refinance after appreciation (BRRRR strategy)
- Wholesale to another investor (assignment strategy)

**Key Analysis Metrics:**

- **Cash-on-Cash Return:** Annual cash flow ÷ Total cash invested
- **Cap Rate:** Annual net operating income ÷ Property value
- **Gross Rent Multiplier:** Purchase price ÷ Annual rental income
- **Debt Service Coverage Ratio:** Monthly rent ÷ Monthly mortgage payment

**Principle #3: Funding is About Systems, Not Net Worth**

Traditional real estate financing focuses on your personal income, assets, and credit history. But business funding focuses on your business's potential for profitability and your ability to service debt.

**The Complete Funding Framework:**

**Traditional Financing (20-25% down):**

- Conventional mortgages for owner-occupied properties (3-5% down)
- Investment property mortgages (20-25% down)
- Portfolio lenders for multiple properties
- Asset-based lenders for unique situations

**Business Credit Funding (0-5% down):**

- Business credit cards for down payments and renovations

- Business lines of credit for working capital
- Equipment financing for property improvements
- SBA loans for larger commercial properties

## Alternative Funding Sources:

- Private money lenders (individuals investing retirement funds)
- Hard money lenders (short-term, asset-based financing)
- Seller financing (owner carries the note)
- Lease options and contract for deed arrangements
- Real estate crowdfunding platforms
- Investment partnerships and joint ventures

## The Credit Card Real Estate Strategy:

1. Apply for business credit cards with 0% promotional APR periods
2. Use cards for down payments, closing costs, and renovation expenses
3. Ensure property cash flow covers minimum credit card payments
4. Pay off balances before promotional periods end
5. Use rewards points for business travel and property research

## Funding Application Timeline:

- Month 1-2: Business entity formation and banking setup
- Month 3-4: First business credit card applications
- Month 5-6: Trade reference establishment and credit building
- Month 7-8: Major bank business credit card applications
- Month 9-12: Business line of credit and larger limit applications

**Principle #4: Property Management is About Systems, Not Time**

The goal of real estate investing is to build passive income, not to create a second full-time job. Proper systems and delegation are essential for scaling beyond a few properties.

**The Property Management Automation Framework:**

**Digital Infrastructure:**

- Online rent collection portals (no checks or cash accepted)
- Digital maintenance request systems
- Automated lease renewal processes
- Electronic document storage and management
- Real-time financial reporting dashboards

**Professional Property Management:**

- Hire property management companies for out-of-area properties
- Establish clear approval limits for different expense categories
- Require monthly financial reports and quarterly strategy meetings
- Use property managers who specialize in your property types and markets

**Tenant Management Systems:**

- Thorough tenant screening processes (credit, background, employment verification)
- Clear lease agreements with specific policies and procedures

- Automated late fee assessment and collection procedures
- Regular property inspections and maintenance schedules

**Financial Management:**

- Separate business bank accounts for each property or market
- Automated expense tracking and categorization
- Regular profit and loss analysis by property
- Annual tax preparation with qualified real estate accountants

**Communication Protocols:**

- Emergency contact procedures (clearly defined emergencies only)
- Weekly operational reports from property managers
- Monthly financial reviews and strategy planning
- Quarterly face-to-face or video conference meetings

## Principle #5: Scaling Requires Geographic and Strategy Diversification

Local markets provide learning opportunities and initial cash flow, but building significant wealth often requires expanding beyond your immediate area to access better opportunities.

**Geographic Expansion Strategy:**

**Market Research Process:**

- Population growth trends and economic diversification
- Job market stability and major employer presence

- Rental demand indicators and vacancy rates
- Property price trends and appreciation potential
- Local laws and regulations affecting real estate investors

**Market Entry Protocol:**

- Visit target markets in person for initial assessment
- Connect with local real estate agents, property managers, and contractors
- Analyze 20+ potential deals before making first purchase
- Start with single-family homes before moving to multi-family properties
- Build local team before expanding significantly in new market

**Strategy Diversification Framework:**

**Buy and Hold Rentals:**

- Focus on cash flow positive properties in stable markets
- Target properties that meet or exceed the 1% rule
- Build portfolio of 10+ properties for significant passive income

**Fix and Flip:**

- Focus on properties needing cosmetic improvements in appreciating markets
- Develop reliable contractor teams and project management systems
- Target 20-30% profit margins after all costs

## Wholesaling:

- Focus on finding deeply discounted properties for other investors
- Build network of cash buyers and fix-and-flip investors
- Target $5,000-$15,000 assignment fees per deal

## Commercial Real Estate:

- Move to apartment buildings, office buildings, or retail properties
- Focus on markets with strong rental demand and growth potential
- Use business credit and investor partnerships for larger down payments

## Principle #6: Wealth Multiplication Through Travel Hacking

Real estate business expenses, when run through the right credit cards, can generate enough rewards points to travel anywhere in the world in first class—essentially turning your business expenses into lifestyle upgrades.

## The Travel Hacking Framework:

## Credit Card Strategy:

- Use business credit cards for all real estate expenses
- Focus on cards with transferable points (Chase, American Express, Capital One)
- Target signup bonuses of 75,000+ points per card
- Use different cards for different expense categories to maximize earnings

**Point Maximization:**

- Real estate purchases: 1-2 points per dollar
- Contractor payments: 2-3 points per dollar (using services like Plastiq)
- Business expenses: 3-5 points per dollar on category bonuses
- Property management fees: 1-2 points per dollar

**Redemption Strategy:**

- Transfer points to airline partners for international business class travel
- Use hotel points for luxury accommodations during property research trips
- Book award travel 6-12 months in advance for best availability
- Combine business travel with property market research

**Annual Travel Budget:** With $100,000+ in annual real estate business expenses, expect to earn:

- 150,000-300,000 credit card points annually
- Enough for 2-4 international business class trips
- Multiple domestic first class trips
- 10-20 nights in luxury hotels

This system essentially makes international travel a business expense that costs points instead of cash, allowing you to research international real estate markets while enjoying luxury travel experiences.

**House Money Hack: The Complete Implementation Timeline**

Here's how to implement the complete House Money system over 18 months:

### Months 1-3: Foundation Building

- Credit repair and optimization
- Business entity formation and banking
- Real estate market research and education
- First business credit card applications

### Months 4-6: First Deal Execution

- Property analysis and offer submission
- Funding coordination and closing preparation
- Property management system setup
- First rental property acquisition

### Months 7-9: System Optimization

- Additional business credit applications
- Property management automation implementation
- Second property acquisition
- Travel rewards optimization

### Months 10-12: Scaling Preparation

- Geographic market expansion research
- Team building in target markets
- Additional funding source development
- Portfolio management systematization

**Months 13-15: Accelerated Growth**

- Multiple property acquisitions
- Advanced funding strategies
- International market exploration
- Digital business development

**Months 16-18: Wealth Multiplication**

- Portfolio optimization and refinancing
- Advanced investment strategies
- Passive income goal achievement
- Freedom lifestyle implementation

**The key is consistent, systematic progress rather than trying to do everything at once.**

Each principle builds on the previous one, creating a compound effect that accelerates your wealth building over time.

**Your credit becomes the foundation for your funding. Your funding enables your real estate acquisitions. Your real estate generates the cash flow that services your funding and creates your passive income. Your passive income buys back your time to scale the entire system.**

**This isn't just a real estate system—it's a freedom system. Where will your house money take you?**

# CHAPTER 12

## The Final Lap

Sitting in my first-class seat on Emirates Flight 217 from Atlanta to Dubai in March 2023, I couldn't help but reflect on the journey that brought me here. The kid who left Longview, Texas with everything he owned in a cardboard box was now flying to check on his international real estate investments, using points earned from business expenses, traveling to a city where Disney World was about to open its newest theme park—and where I owned property that would benefit from that massive development.

But this wasn't just another business trip. This was a pilgrimage of sorts, a chance to see how far the principles I'd learned could take someone willing to run their own race.

### The Numbers That Changed Everything

As I reviewed my portfolio summary on the flight, the numbers still seemed surreal:

- 31 rental properties across 2 countries generating $28,500 monthly cash flow

- Business credit capacity of over $800,000 across multiple banking relationships
- Digital education business generating $75,000+ per month in recurring revenue
- Real estate portfolio value exceeding $4.2 million with minimal personal capital invested
- Travel rewards earned: over 2.3 million points lifetime, enabling 47 international trips

But the most important number wasn't financial—it was the 500+ high school athletes I'd coached over 17 years, many of whom had gone on to college and were now implementing the financial principles I'd taught them during those long training runs.

**The Dubai Lesson**

Walking through Dubai Marina, looking up at the building where I owned a luxury apartment, I was struck by how this investment represented everything I'd learned about thinking globally while executing systematically.

When I first purchased this property in 2024 for $250,000, using business credit cards for the down payment and installments, people thought I was crazy. "Why are you buying property in a place you've never lived, in a country you don't understand?"

But I understood something more important: **good deals transcend geography**.

The fundamentals were solid:

- Strong economic growth and population influx
- Limited supply of luxury waterfront properties
- Developer financing that allowed creative funding strategies
- Rental yields that exceeded U.S. market averages
- Currency diversification that provided hedge against dollar fluctuations

A couple years later, that property was worth $350,000 and generating $4,200 per month in rental income. The credit cards I'd used for the purchase had been paid off within three years using rental income and business profits.

More importantly, that investment had opened my eyes to global opportunities that domestic-only investors never see.

## The Disney Announcement

During this trip, Disney had just announced that UAE would be home to their newest international theme park, opening in 2026. Property values in my area were already up 15% just from the announcement.

This wasn't luck—it was the result of understanding that emerging markets often provide opportunities that mature markets can't offer. Dubai had been building infrastructure, attracting international businesses, and positioning itself as a global hub for over two decades. The Disney announcement was just the latest validation of that strategy.

## The Coach's Perspective

Flying back to Atlanta, I thought about the conversation I'd had with my track team before leaving for Dubai. They'd asked, as they always did, about my trips and my business.

"Coach P," one of my seniors had said, "how do you know when to take risks like buying property in another country?"

It was a great question, and it gave me a chance to connect the lessons they were learning on the track to the principles they'd need for building wealth.

"Remember when you first started training for the 5K? You couldn't run one mile without stopping. But you didn't try to run five miles on day one, right? You built up gradually—two miles, then three, then four, then five."

"Real estate is the same way. I didn't start by buying property in Dubai. I started with a small house in Athens that I could understand, manage, and afford. Then I bought another one. Then I learned about business credit. Then I bought properties in other states. Each deal taught me something that prepared me for the next level."

"The 'risk' of buying in Dubai wasn't really a risk by the time I did it, because I'd already proven the system worked on smaller deals. I understood how to analyze properties, how to fund purchases, how to manage rentals, and how to use credit strategically."

"The biggest risk would have been staying small when I had the knowledge and systems to go bigger."

## The Patience Principle

One thing coaching had taught me that business books never could was the power of patience combined with persistent action.

Watching 14-year-old kids develop into 18-year-old scholarship athletes over four years taught me that meaningful results require time horizons longer than most people are willing to commit to.

The same principle applied to wealth building. My real estate portfolio hadn't been built in a year or even three years. It had been built over fifteen years of consistent application of proven principles.

Every deal built on the knowledge from previous deals. Every credit application built on the history from previous applications. Every property management system improvement built on lessons learned from previous challenges.

**The compound effect of small, consistent actions over long time periods creates results that seem impossible to people who only see the end result.**

## The Freedom Reality

But what did financial freedom actually look like in practice?

**Time Freedom:** I could coach high school track without worrying about missing work. I could travel for weeks without business operations suffering. I could pursue new opportunities without being constrained by cash flow needs.

**Location Freedom:** I could work from anywhere with internet access. My business operated in multiple time zones without requiring my presence in any specific location.

**Choice Freedom:** I could say no to opportunities that didn't align with my values or goals, because I wasn't dependent on any single income source.

**Impact Freedom:** I could spend time teaching, mentoring, and creating content because my passive income covered my living expenses.

This wasn't retirement—it was the ability to choose how to spend my time based on purpose rather than necessity.

## The Generational Impact

Perhaps the most meaningful aspect of this journey was understanding that wealth building isn't just about personal freedom—it's about creating generational change.

I thought about the land I owned back in Longview, Texas. Twenty acres that my grandparents could never have imagined their grandson owning. Land that could eventually be developed, sold, or passed down to future generations.

I thought about the kids I'd coached who were now in college, avoiding the credit card debt and financial mistakes that trap so many young adults, because they understood the difference between assets and liabilities.

I thought about my parents' house in Texas, which I'd been able to pay off using cash flow from my real estate investments. They'd worked their entire lives, and now they could live without the stress of mortgage payments.

I thought about my brother's house, which I'd helped him purchase using strategies I'd learned about credit and funding.

**Wealth, properly built, creates ripples that extend far beyond the wealth builder.**

### The Five-Year Vision

Looking ahead, I could see the next phase of my journey clearly:

**Real Estate Expansion:** Target 50 total rental units across 6 countries, focusing on emerging markets with strong growth potential and favorable investment structures.

**Digital Business Scaling:** Grow the Credit to Real Estate education business to serve 10,000+ students annually through courses, coaching, and live events.

**Coaching Evolution:** Develop a formal program that teaches financial literacy and entrepreneurship to high school athletes nationwide.

**International Consulting:** Help other American investors navigate international real estate markets safely and profitably.

**Legacy Building:** Establish scholarship funds and mentorship programs that give other young people from small towns the exposure and opportunities that changed my life.

### The 47-Year-Old Perspective

People are always surprised when I tell them I'm 47. They expect someone my age to look more worn down, more stressed, more tired. But building wealth the right way—through systems rather than grinding—actually makes you younger.

I sleep better knowing my income isn't dependent on my daily effort. I exercise more because I have time for it. I travel more because I can afford it and because I earn points doing business I'd be doing anyway. I'm more patient because I understand that compound returns reward long-term thinking.

**Age becomes an advantage when you understand that time is the most powerful factor in wealth building.**

Starting at 25 and building slowly but systematically beat starting at 35 and trying to build quickly through high-risk strategies.

## The Running Metaphor Completed

As I finished writing this chapter, I was preparing for my afternoon run—still six miles, still six days a week, still using that time to think through business decisions and life priorities.

The metaphor that had guided my entire journey remained as relevant as ever: **running your own race.**

In track, success isn't about beating everyone else—it's about running your best time. It's about consistent training, smart strategy, and long-term improvement.

In wealth building, success isn't about having more than everyone else—it's about creating the life you actually want. It's about consistent habits, smart systems, and long-term thinking.

The kid who got on the Greyhound bus with everything he owned in a box was running toward something he couldn't fully see. He just knew he had to get started, had to keep moving, had to trust that the path would become clearer as he ran.

Thirty years later, I'm still running. The path has led places I never could have imagined—from Garden City, Kansas to Dubai Marina, from welfare vegetables to first-class flights, from uncertain futures to generational wealth.

But the principles remain the same: **Start where you are. Use what you have. Do what you can. Keep running.**

**House Money Hack: Your Race Starts Now**

The most important lesson from my entire journey is this: **the best time to start building wealth was 20 years ago. The second best time is today.**

Every day you wait is compound growth you're giving up. Every month you delay is cash flow you're not earning. Every year you postpone is freedom you're not experiencing.

But here's the beautiful thing about the House Money system: **it works regardless of when you start.**

Whether you're 22 or 52, whether you have perfect credit or damaged credit, whether you have $50,000 saved or $500 in your checking account, the principles remain the same:

Fix and optimize your credit systematically

Establish business credit parallel to personal credit

Learn to analyze real estate deals based on numbers, not emotions

Use other people's money to fund your investments

Build systems that create passive income without constant involvement

Scale geographically and strategically over time

Turn business expenses into lifestyle upgrades through travel hacking

Find purpose beyond profit to sustain long-term success

The timeline might be different based on your starting point, but the destination is the same: **financial freedom that allows you to live life on your terms.**

**Your race starts the moment you decide to start running.**

You don't need to see the finish line to take the first step. You don't need to have perfect conditions to begin. You just need to start moving in the right direction with the right system.

The track is open. Your running shoes are waiting. The only question is: **Are you ready to run your own race?**

**Your house money journey begins now. Where will it take you?**

# CHAPTER 13

## Your Starting Line

If you've made it this far in my story, you're probably asking yourself the same question I asked when I first heard about using business credit for real estate: "This sounds too good to be true. Does this really work for regular people, or just for someone like Lee who had lucky timing?"

Let me be clear about something: there was nothing lucky about my timing, and there's nothing special about me that you don't have access to.

I wasn't born with perfect credit—I had to rebuild mine from 580. I wasn't born with money—I started with everything I owned in a cardboard box. I wasn't born with real estate knowledge—I learned it running six miles a day with someone who was willing to teach me. I wasn't born with business credit—I learned that system from a mentor who saw potential in me.

Everything I accomplished, you can accomplish. The principles haven't changed. The opportunities haven't disappeared. The system still works.

But there's a difference between reading about a system and implementing it. And that difference determines whether this book becomes inspiration or transformation in your life.

## The Three Types of People

In my years of teaching this system through courses, coaching, and the five-day challenge, I've learned that people generally fall into three categories when they encounter new information:

**The Skeptics** (70%): These people look for reasons why something won't work for them. They focus on obstacles instead of opportunities. They say things like "That might work for other people, but my situation is different" or "I don't have enough money/time/credit to get started."

**The Researchers** (25%): These people love learning about new strategies but struggle with implementation. They buy courses, attend seminars, read books, and can analyze deals all day long. But they never actually pull the trigger on their first property because they're always waiting to learn "just one more thing."

**The Implementers** (5%): These people learn enough to get started, then figure out the rest as they go. They're not afraid of making mistakes because they understand that experience is the best teacher. They take action even when they don't feel 100% ready.

**Which category do you want to be in?**

## Starting Where You Are

One of the most common questions I get is: "Lee, what if my credit is terrible?" or "What if I don't have any money saved?" or "What if I live in an expensive market where real estate doesn't cash flow?"

Here's the truth: **every successful real estate investor started with limitations.**

My credit was terrible when I started. I had limited savings. I was living in a college town where most investors said you couldn't make money with traditional rental properties.

But I didn't let those limitations define what was possible. Instead, I used them as my starting point and worked systematically to improve my situation.

**If your credit is terrible:** Start with credit repair. It takes 6-12 months to see significant improvement, but that time is going to pass whether you're working on your credit or not. You might as well be improving it.

**If you don't have money saved:** Start by learning the system and building your credit while you save. Focus on increasing your income and decreasing your expenses. Look for wholesaling opportunities that don't require capital.

**If you live in an expensive market:** Start by learning to analyze deals, even if you can't afford to buy in your local market yet. Research other markets where properties do cash flow. Consider house hacking or starting with smaller properties.

**The key is to start where you are, not where you wish you were.**

### The 90-Day Action Plan

Based on working with thousands of students, here's the most effective way to implement the House Money system in your first 90 days:

## Days 1-30: Foundation Building

*Week 1: Credit Assessment*

- Pull all three credit reports (Experian, Equifax, TransUnion)
- List every negative item, outstanding debt, and improvement opportunity
- Calculate current utilization ratios on all credit cards
- Set up automatic payments for all current accounts

*Week 2: Business Entity Formation*

- Research business entity types and choose LLC or Corporation
- File formation documents with your state
- Apply for EIN (Employer Identification Number) with IRS
- Research business banking options and requirements

*Week 3: Market Research*

- Choose primary market for real estate investing (local or out-of-state)
- Research average property prices, rental rates, and market trends
- Find 3-5 real estate agents who work with investors
- Join local real estate investment groups or online communities

*Week 4: Education and Planning*

- Complete real estate analysis training (online courses or books)
- Practice analyzing 10 real properties using proper metrics
- Create 12-month action plan with specific milestones
- Set up systems for tracking progress and opportunities

## Days 31-60: System Implementation

*Week 5-6: Credit Optimization*

- Dispute any inaccurate information on credit reports
- Pay down credit card balances to below 30% utilization
- Negotiate payment plans or settlements for outstanding debts
- Apply for credit limit increases on existing cards

*Week 7-8: Business Credit Foundation*

- Open business bank account with initial deposit
- Apply for business phone line and professional address
- Establish trade references with vendors that report to business credit bureaus
- Apply for first business credit card with regional bank

*Week 9: Deal Analysis Practice*

- Analyze 20 properties in your target market
- Submit offers on 2-3 properties (even if financing isn't ready yet)
- Build relationships with agents, contractors, and property managers
- Attend local real estate networking events

## Days 61-90: First Deal Execution

*Week 10-11: Funding Preparation*

- Apply for additional business credit cards with major banks
- Organize all financial documents and business records

- Research alternative funding sources (private lenders, hard money)
- Calculate total available capital for first investment

*Week 12: First Property Acquisition*

- Submit serious offers on best deals identified
- Coordinate funding for accepted offer
- Complete due diligence and property inspections
- Close on first rental property

*Week 13: Systems Setup*

- Implement property management systems and automation
- Set up rental collection and tenant screening processes
- Establish maintenance and contractor relationships
- Create financial tracking and reporting systems

**The Common Pitfalls (And How to Avoid Them)**

After teaching this system to thousands of people, I've seen the same mistakes repeated over and over. Here are the most common pitfalls and how to avoid them:

**Pitfall #1: Analysis Paralysis** *The Problem:* Spending months analyzing deals without ever making an offer. *The Solution:* Set a goal to analyze 20 properties, then make offers on the best 3. Learning happens through action, not just analysis.

**Pitfall #2: Credit Card Abuse** *The Problem:* Using business credit cards for personal expenses or lifestyle inflation. *The Solution:* Only use business credit for legitimate business expenses. Set up automatic payments and track every purchase.

**Pitfall #3: Skipping Property Management** *The Problem:* Trying to manage everything yourself to save money. *The Solution:* Factor property management costs into your analysis from the beginning. Your time is valuable—protect it.

**Pitfall #4: Emotional Decision Making** *The Problem:* Buying properties based on how they look or feel rather than how they perform financially. *The Solution:* Never buy a property that doesn't meet your financial criteria, regardless of how much you like it.

**Pitfall #5: Inadequate Reserves** *The Problem:* Using all available credit and cash for deals, leaving no cushion for unexpected expenses. *The Solution:* Always maintain 3-6 months of expenses in reserve and leave some credit capacity unused.

**The Mindset Shifts That Matter**

Success with the House Money system requires more than just tactical knowledge—it requires fundamental shifts in how you think about money, credit, and opportunity.

**From Scarcity to Abundance** Instead of thinking "I can't afford that," start thinking "How can I afford that?" The answer often involves using systems and leverage rather than just saving cash.

**From Consumer to Investor** Instead of using credit for consumption (clothes, cars, vacations), use credit for investments (properties, business assets, income-producing activities).

**From Local to Global** Instead of limiting yourself to your immediate geographic area, think about where the best opportunities exist and how you can access them.

**From Perfectionism to Progress** Instead of waiting until you have perfect credit, perfect knowledge, or perfect timing, start with what you have and improve as you go.

**From Employee to Entrepreneur** Instead of thinking about trading time for money, start thinking about building assets that generate income without your constant involvement.

## The Support System

One of the biggest advantages you have today that I didn't have when I started is access to community and support systems.

When I was learning this stuff, I had to figure it out mostly on my own or through individual mentors like Marcus and David. Today, there are communities, courses, coaching programs, and resources that can accelerate your learning dramatically.

**Take advantage of these resources:**

- Join local real estate investment meetups in your area
- Find an accountability partner who's also implementing this system
- Consider working with experienced mentors who have successfully used these strategies
- Connect with other investors through online communities and forums

- Attend real estate investing seminars and conferences to expand your network

## The Compound Effect of Getting Started

Here's something most people don't understand about wealth building: **the sooner you start, the less you have to contribute to reach the same goals.**

If you start investing $500 per month at age 25 and earn 8% annual returns, you'll have $1.4 million by age 65 after contributing $240,000 total.

If you wait until age 35 to start, you'd need to invest $1,100 per month to reach the same $1.4 million, contributing $396,000 total.

If you wait until age 45, you'd need to invest $2,800 per month to reach the same goal, contributing $672,000 total.

**Time is the most powerful factor in wealth building, and it's the one factor you can't buy back.**

Every month you delay starting costs you compound growth that can never be recovered.

## Your Personal Declaration

If you're ready to stop reading and start implementing, I want you to make a personal declaration—not to me, but to yourself.

Write this down somewhere you'll see it every day:

*"I commit to implementing the House Money system over the next 90 days. I will fix my credit, establish business credit, learn to analyze real estate deals, and acquire my first investment property. I understand that success requires action, not just knowledge, and I'm willing to learn as I go rather than waiting for perfect conditions."*

*"I choose to run my own race at my own pace, focused on my own goals, without comparing my progress to anyone else's timeline."*

*"I believe that if Lee Patterson can go from a cardboard box on a Greyhound bus to international real estate investments, I can achieve financial freedom using the same principles and systems."*

*"My wealth-building journey starts today."*

Sign it. Date it. Keep it somewhere you'll see it when motivation runs low or when obstacles seem overwhelming.

## The Starting Line

Twenty-eight years ago, I stepped onto a Greyhound bus in Longview, Texas with everything I owned in a cardboard box and a dream of something better.

I didn't know exactly where I was going or how I would get there. I just knew I had to start moving toward something bigger than my current situation.

Today, you're standing at your own starting line. You have everything you need to begin:

- The knowledge of how the system works

- The blueprint for implementing it systematically
- The understanding that it's been proven by thousands of others
- The awareness that your current situation doesn't determine your future potential

The only question remaining is: **Are you ready to start running?**

**Your house money journey begins with the next action you take. What will that action be?**

**Ready to take the first step? The same principles that took me from a cardboard box to international real estate investments are available to anyone willing to learn and implement them systematically.**

**Your future self is waiting for you to begin. Don't keep them waiting any longer.**

# CONCLUSION

# Keep Running

As I finish writing this book, I'm sitting on the same track where I first met Mike fifteen years ago. It's 6 AM, the sun is just coming up over Athens, and I'm about to start my daily six-mile run—the same routine that's grounded me through every stage of this journey.

The track looks the same as it did when I was a broke former college athlete trying to figure out what came next. But everything else has changed.

Where I once saw limitations, I now see possibilities. Where I once felt constrained by my circumstances, I now understand that circumstances are just starting points. Where I once thought wealth was for other people, I now know that anyone can build it with the right system and enough persistence.

## The Race Never Ends

People often ask me when I'll "retire" from real estate investing, when I'll stop building the business, when I'll be satisfied with what I've achieved.

The truth is, I hope I never stop. Not because I need more money, but because I've learned that growth and contribution give life meaning in ways that accumulation alone never can.

The race isn't about reaching some final destination where you can stop running. It's about continuing to move forward, continuing to learn, continuing to help others discover what they're capable of achieving.

Every property I acquire teaches me something new. Every student I coach shows me a different perspective. Every challenge I overcome proves that there's always another level of growth possible.

## What I Know Now

If I could go back and talk to that 18-year-old kid boarding the Greyhound bus in Longview, Texas, here's what I'd tell him:

**Trust the process.** Even when you can't see where the path is leading, keep taking the next step. Every experience—good and bad—is preparing you for opportunities you can't yet imagine.

**Systems beat motivation.** Motivation gets you started, but systems keep you going when motivation fades. Focus on building habits and processes that work whether you feel like doing them or not.

**Credit is a tool, not a trap.** Used properly, credit becomes one of your most powerful wealth-building tools. Used improperly, it can destroy your financial future. Learn the difference and respect the power.

**Real estate is forgiving.** If you buy in decent areas, run the numbers conservatively, and hold for reasonable time periods, real estate investing is one of the most forgiving ways to build wealth. You'll make mistakes, but good properties in good areas tend to work out over time.

**Geography is not destiny.** Your zip code doesn't determine your net worth. In today's connected world, you can invest anywhere, learn from anyone, and build wealth regardless of where you start.

**Teaching amplifies everything.** When you help others succeed, you don't just multiply your impact—you deepen your own understanding and create opportunities you never would have discovered on your own.

**Purpose matters more than profit.** Money without meaning is just scorekeeping. Find ways to use your wealth-building journey to serve something bigger than yourself.

**The compound effect is real.** Small, consistent actions over long periods create results that seem impossible to people who only see the end result. Trust the math of compound growth.

**Your story matters.** Whatever your background, whatever your starting point, whatever challenges you've faced—your journey can inspire and educate others who are facing similar obstacles.

**The race is long.** You have time to figure it out, time to recover from mistakes, time to build the life you really want. Don't rush. Don't panic. Just keep moving forward.

## What You Can Do Right Now

As you close this book and think about your next steps, remember that knowledge without action is just entertainment. The difference between people who build wealth and people who just read about building wealth is what they do in the 24 hours after finishing the last page.

Here's what I want you to do today:

**Pull your credit reports.** You can't improve what you don't measure. Order your reports from all three bureaus and create a plan for optimization.

**Choose your first market.** Whether it's your local area or a market you've researched, pick one place to focus your initial efforts.

**Analyze your first deal.** Find a property listing and run the numbers using the 1% rule and cash flow analysis. It doesn't matter if you can't afford it yet—practice the process.

**Start building your team.** Identify a real estate agent, property manager, contractor, and lender who work with investors in your target market.

**Set your timeline.** Create a realistic 12-month plan for acquiring your first investment property. Break it down into quarterly and monthly milestones.

Most importantly, **start running your own race.**

Stop comparing your chapter 1 to someone else's chapter 20. Stop waiting for perfect conditions. Stop making excuses about why it won't work for you.

## The Starting Line is Wherever You Are

The beautiful thing about the House Money system is that it works regardless of your starting point. I've seen it work for college students and retirees, for people with perfect credit and people rebuilding from bankruptcy, for people with six-figure incomes and people making minimum wage.

The timeline might be different. The specific tactics might vary. But the principles remain the same:

- Build and leverage credit systematically
- Analyze deals based on numbers, not emotions
- Use other people's money to fund your investments
- Create passive income through smart property management
- Scale geographically and strategically over time
- Turn business expenses into lifestyle experiences
- Find purpose that extends beyond personal profit

**Your race starts the moment you decide to start running.**

## The View from Here

As I lace up my running shoes and head out for my morning miles, I'm grateful for the journey that brought me to this point. From that cardboard box to international real estate investments, from student debt to financial freedom, from uncertainty to purpose.

But I'm even more excited about what comes next. The properties I haven't bought yet. The students I haven't taught yet. The opportunities I haven't discovered yet. The impact I haven't made yet.

Because the race never ends—it just keeps getting more interesting.

The track is open. Your running shoes are waiting. The only question is: **Are you ready to start running?**

**Your house money journey begins with the first step you take after closing this book.**

**What will that step be?**

**Keep running,**
**Lee A. Patterson**
**Athens, Georgia**

# APPENDICES

## APPENDIX A: CREDIT REPAIR CHECKLIST

### Phase 1: Credit Assessment (Week 1)

☐ **Order Credit Reports**

- Experian: www.experian.com
- Equifax: www.equifax.com
- TransUnion: www.transunion.com
- Review each report for accuracy and completeness

☐ **Document Everything**

- List all accounts (open and closed)
- Note all negative items (late payments, collections, charge-offs)
- Calculate current utilization ratios on all credit cards
- Identify any inaccurate or outdated information

☐ **Create Master Improvement Plan**

- Prioritize items by impact on credit score

- Set target credit score goal
- Establish 90-day action timeline

## Phase 2: Dispute Process (Weeks 2-4)

☐ **Dispute Letter Template**

[Date]
[Credit Bureau Address]

RE: Request for Investigation - [Your Name], SSN: XXX-XX-[Last 4 digits]

Dear Sir/Madam,

I am writing to dispute the following information on my credit report. The items I am disputing are encircled on the attached copy of my credit report.

Account: [Account Name/Number]
Reason for Dispute: [Inaccurate/Incomplete/Unverified]

Please investigate and remove or correct this information as soon as possible.

Sincerely,
[Your Signature]
[Your Printed Name]

☐ **Required Documentation**

- Copy of credit report with disputed items circled
- Copy of government-issued ID
- Proof of address (utility bill, bank statement)
- Supporting documentation for disputes

☐ **Follow-Up Process**

- Send disputes via certified mail with return receipt
- Track 30-day investigation timeline
- Review updated credit reports after investigation
- Re-dispute if necessary

## Phase 3: Debt Management (Weeks 3-8)

☐ **Contact Creditors**

- List all outstanding debts with contact information
- Negotiate payment plans for past-due accounts
- Request "pay for delete" agreements in writing
- Get all agreements in writing before making payments

☐ **Utilization Optimization**

- Pay down credit card balances to below 30% utilization
- Target balances below 10% for maximum score impact
- Request credit limit increases on existing cards
- Consider balance transfers to optimize utilization

## Phase 4: Ongoing Maintenance

☐ **Payment Automation**

- Set up automatic payments for all accounts
- Schedule payments 2-3 days before due dates
- Monitor account statements monthly
- Never miss a payment going forward

☐ **Regular Monitoring**

- Check credit scores monthly (free through credit card apps)
- Review credit reports quarterly
- Update credit monitoring alerts
- Track progress toward target score

# APPENDIX B: BUSINESS FORMATION TEMPLATES

## Business Entity Comparison Chart

| Feature | LLC | S-Corp | C-Corp |
|---|---|---|---|
| Formation Complexity | Simple | Moderate | Complex |
| Tax Treatment | Pass-through | Pass-through | Double taxation |
| Ownership Restrictions | None | Limited | None |
| Best For Real Estate | ✓ | Limited | Limited |
| Business Credit Building | ✓ | ✓ | ✓ |

# LLC Formation Checklist

## ☐ Pre-Formation

- Choose business name (check availability in your state)
- Select registered agent (yourself or service company)
- Determine business address
- Research state filing fees and requirements

## ☐ Formation Documents

- File Articles of Organization with state
- Create Operating Agreement (even for single-member LLCs)
- Apply for EIN with IRS (Form SS-4)
- Register with state tax authority if required

## ☐ Post-Formation Setup

- Open business bank account
- Apply for business phone line
- Set up business address (not home address)
- Order business cards and basic marketing materials
- Register with business credit bureaus

# Sample Operating Agreement Provisions

**Business Purpose:** "The purpose of this LLC is to engage in real estate investment activities including but not limited to: acquiring, holding, managing, improving, and disposing of real property for investment purposes."

**Management Structure:** "This LLC shall be managed by its members. All major business decisions requiring expenditures over $[amount] shall require approval of [percentage]% of membership interests."

**Capital Contributions:** "Initial capital contributions are not required. Members may make additional capital contributions as needed for business operations."

## EIN Application Process

☐ **Online Application (Recommended)**

- Visit www.irs.gov and search "Apply for EIN"
- Complete Form SS-4 online
- Receive EIN immediately upon completion
- Save confirmation letter for records

☐ **Required Information**

- Legal business name
- Business address
- Responsible party name and SSN
- Business structure type
- Reason for applying
- Business start date

# APPENDIX C: REAL ESTATE ANALYSIS WORKSHEETS

## Property Analysis Worksheet

**Property Information:**

- Address: _____
- List Price: $_____
- Square Footage: _____
- Bedrooms/Bathrooms: ____
- Year Built: _____
- Property Type: _____

**Income Analysis:**

- Market Rent: $_____/month
- Less Vacancy (5-10%): $_____
- Less Property Management (8-12%): $_____

**Net Rental Income: $_____/month**

**Expense Analysis:**

- Property Taxes: $_____/month
- Insurance: $_____/month
- Maintenance (5-10% of rent): $_____/month
- Capital Improvements (5% of rent): $_____/month
- Other expenses: $_____/month

- **Total Monthly Expenses: $_____**

**Financing Analysis:**

- Purchase Price: $_____
- Down Payment (20-25%): $_____
- Loan Amount: $_____
- Interest Rate: _____%
- Loan Term: _____ years
- **Monthly Payment (P&I): $_____**

**Cash Flow Analysis:**

- Net Rental Income: $_____
- Less Total Expenses: $(_____)
- Less Mortgage Payment: $(_____)
- **Monthly Cash Flow: $_____**

**Investment Returns:**

- Total Cash Invested: $_____
- Annual Cash Flow: $_____ (Monthly × 12)
- **Cash-on-Cash Return:** _____% (Annual Cash Flow ÷ Cash Invested)

## The 1% Rule Quick Check

**Formula:** Monthly Rent ÷ Purchase Price = _____%

- **Above 1.0%** = Likely positive cash flow ✓

- **0.7% - 1.0%** = Marginal deal, analyze carefully
- **Below 0.7%** = Likely negative cash flow X

## Comparable Sales Analysis

| Address | Sale Price | Price/SqFt | Days on Market | Sale Date |
|---------|-----------|------------|----------------|-----------|
| | $ | $ | | |
| | $ | $ | | |
| | $ | $ | | |
| Average | $ | $ | | |

## Comparable Rent Analysis

| Address | Monthly Rent | Rent/SqFt | Bedrooms | Amenities |
|---------|-------------|-----------|----------|-----------|
| | $ | $ | | |
| | $ | $ | | |
| | $ | $ | | |
| Average | $ | $ | | |

## Rehab Cost Estimator

**Cosmetic Updates:**

- Paint (interior): $2-4 per sq ft
- Paint (exterior): $3-6 per sq ft
- Flooring (carpet): $3-8 per sq ft

- Flooring (hardwood): $8-15 per sq ft
- Light fixtures: $100-500 each
- Cabinet hardware: $5-25 per piece

## Major Systems:

- HVAC replacement: $5,000-15,000
- Roof replacement: $8,000-20,000
- Electrical update: $3,000-8,000
- Plumbing update: $3,000-10,000
- Windows replacement: $300-800 each

**Always add 20% contingency to rehab estimates**

# APPENDIX D: TRAVEL HACKING CREDIT CARD GUIDE

## Top Business Credit Cards for Real Estate Investors

### Chase Ink Business Cash

- Sign-up bonus: 75,000 points after $7,500 spend
- 0% APR: 12 months on purchases
- Rewards: 5% on office supplies, 2% on gas/restaurants, 1% everything else
- Annual fee: $0
- Best for: First business card, ongoing business expenses

### American Express Business Gold

- Sign-up bonus: 130,000 points after $10,000 spend
- 0% APR: 12 months on purchases
- Rewards: 4x on top spending categories, 1x everything else
- Annual fee: $295
- Best for: High spenders, travel rewards

### Capital One Spark Cash

- Sign-up bonus: $1,000 cash after $10,000 spend
- 0% APR: 12 months on purchases
- Rewards: 2% cash back on everything
- Annual fee: $95
- Best for: Simple rewards, consistent cash back

### Wells Fargo Business Platinum

- Sign-up bonus: $500 cash after $5,000 spend
- 0% APR: 18 months on purchases
- Rewards: 1.5% cash back on everything
- Annual fee: $0
- Best for: Long 0% period, no annual fee

## Point Transfer Partners

### Chase Ultimate Rewards:

- United Airlines: 1:1 transfer
- Southwest Airlines: 1:1 transfer

- Hyatt Hotels: 1:1 transfer
- World of Hyatt: 1:1 transfer

## American Express Membership Rewards:

- Delta Airlines: 1:1 transfer
- Emirates: 1:1 transfer
- Hilton Hotels: 1:2 transfer
- Marriott: 1:1 transfer

## Capital One Miles:

- Turkish Airlines: 1:1 transfer
- Emirates: 1:1 transfer
- Wyndham Hotels: 1:1 transfer
- Choice Hotels: 1:1 transfer

# Sweet Spot Redemptions

## Business Class to Europe:

- Turkish Airlines: 45,000 miles
- Air France: 50,000 miles
- United: 70,000 miles

## Business Class to Asia:

- ANA: 75,000 miles
- Singapore Airlines: 85,000 miles
- Emirates: 100,000 miles

**Luxury Hotels:**

- Hyatt: 15,000-40,000 points/night
- Marriott: 35,000-85,000 points/night
- Hilton: 40,000-120,000 points/night

# Credit Card Application Strategy

**Month 1:** Apply for first business card (start with regional bank) **Month 3:** Apply for Chase business card **Month 5:** Apply for American Express business card **Month 7:** Apply for Capital One business card **Month 9:** Apply for additional Chase card (if under 5/24 rule) **Month 11:** Apply for specialized card based on spending patterns

**Important Rules:**

- Never apply for more than one card per month
- Chase 5/24 rule: Won't approve if you've opened 5+ personal cards in 24 months
- Business cards typically don't count toward 5/24
- Always have legitimate business purpose and expenses

# Point Earning Strategies

**Real Estate Purchases:**

- Down payments: 1-2x points
- Closing costs: 1-2x points
- Contractor payments (via Plastiq): 2.85% fee, 1x points
- Property management: 1x points

**Business Expenses:**

- Office supplies: Up to 5x points
- Advertising/marketing: Up to 4x points
- Shipping: Up to 5x points
- Phone/internet: Up to 5x points

**Manufactured Spending (Advanced):**

- Gift card purchases at office supply stores: 5x points
- Money orders for bill payments: Varies
- Bank account funding: Varies by bank

**Always ensure spending is for legitimate business purposes and track for tax deductions**

# APPENDIX E: RESOURCES AND NEXT STEPS

## Real Estate Analysis Tools

**Free Tools:**

- BiggerPockets Calculator: biggerpockets.com/calc
- Zillow Rent Estimates: zillow.com/rental-manager
- Rentometer: rentometer.com
- City-data.com: Local market demographics

**Paid Tools:**

- RentSpree: rentspree.com
- PropertyRadar: propertyradar.com
- RealtyMogul: realtymogul.com
- Mashvisor: mashvisor.com

## Credit Monitoring Services

**Free Options:**

- Credit Karma: creditkarma.com
- Credit Sesame: creditsesame.com
- Annual Credit Report: annualcreditreport.com
- Bank/credit card free scores

**Paid Options:**

- Experian Premium: experian.com
- MyFICO: myfico.com
- IdentityGuard: identityguard.com

## Business Credit Resources

**Business Credit Bureaus:**

- Dun & Bradstreet: dnb.com
- Experian Business: experian.com/business
- Equifax Business: equifax.com/business

**Trade Reference Vendors:**

- Uline (office supplies): uline.com
- Grainger (maintenance supplies): grainger.com
- Home Depot Pro (contractor supplies): homedepot.com/c/pro
- Fleet cards (gas): Shell, BP, Exxon business cards

## Property Management Software

**Beginner-Friendly:**

- Rentals.com: rentals.com
- TurboTenant: turbotenant.com
- Avail: avail.co
- Cozy (now part of Apartments.com): apartments.com

**Advanced Platforms:**

- AppFolio: appfolio.com
- Buildium: buildium.com
- Rent Manager: rentmanager.com
- Yardi: yardi.com

## Legal and Tax Resources

**Legal:**

- LegalZoom: legalzoom.com (basic documents)
- Rocket Lawyer: rocketlawyer.com (basic documents)

- Local real estate attorney (for complex transactions)
- State bar association referral services

**Tax Professionals:**

- CPA specializing in real estate
- Enrolled Agent (EA) credential
- TurboTax Business (self-preparation)
- Tax preparation software for real estate

# Continuing Education

**Books:**

- "The Book on Rental Property Investing" by Brandon Turner
- "Buy, Rehab, Rent, Refinance, Repeat" by David Greene
- "The Millionaire Real Estate Investor" by Gary Keller
- "Rich Dad Poor Dad" by Robert Kiyosaki

**Podcasts:**

- BiggerPockets Real Estate Podcast
- Real Estate Rookie Podcast
- The Real Estate Guys
- Best Real Estate Investing Advice Ever

**Online Communities:**

- BiggerPockets.com forums
- Facebook real estate investor groups

- Reddit: r/RealEstate, r/realestateinvesting
- Local REIA (Real Estate Investment Association) meetings

# Market Research Resources

### Demographics and Economics:

- Census.gov: Population and economic data
- BLS.gov: Bureau of Labor Statistics employment data
- Fred.stlouisfed.org: Economic data and trends
- City-data.com: Local market information

### Real Estate Market Data:

- Realtor.com market trends
- Zillow market reports
- RentData.org: Rental market information
- Local MLS market reports

# International Real Estate

### Dubai Resources:

- Dubai Land Department: dubailand.gov.ae
- RERA (Real Estate Regulatory Agency): rera.ae
- Major developers: Emaar, DAMAC, Nakheel
- Property portals: Bayut.com, Property Finder

## General International:

- Global Property Guide: globalpropertyguide.com
- International Real Estate Federation: fiabci.org
- Local real estate law firms in target countries
- Tax treaty information: IRS Publication 901

# Emergency Contact Information

## Credit Bureaus Fraud Departments:

- Experian: 1-888-397-3742
- Equifax: 1-800-525-6285
- TransUnion: 1-800-680-7289

## Federal Trade Commission:

- Identity theft reports: identitytheft.gov
- Consumer complaints: consumer.ftc.gov
- Phone: 1-877-FTC-HELP

## IRS Business Support:

- Business tax questions: 1-800-829-4933
- EIN verification: 1-800-829-4933
- Form SS-4 help: irs.gov/businesses

# Action Steps Checklist

**Week 1:**

- Order all three credit reports
- Research business entity formation in your state
- Choose target real estate market
- Set up basic tracking spreadsheets

**Week 2:**

- Create credit improvement plan
- File business formation documents
- Contact 3 real estate agents in target market
- Start analyzing first properties

**Week 3:**

- Apply for EIN
- Open business bank account
- Submit first property offers
- Research property management companies

**Week 4:**

- Apply for first business credit card
- Set up business phone and address
- Join local real estate investment group
- Create 90-day action plan

**Remember: Progress over perfection. Start where you are, use what you have, do what you can.**